WHY AM I SO ANGRY? MY SEARCH FOR THE TRUTH

HELEN GERONDIS

BALBOA.
PRESS
A DIVISION OF HAY HOUSE

Balboa Press books may be ordered through booksellers or by contacting:

Balboa Press
A Division of Hay House
1663 Liberty Drive
Bloomington, IN 47403
www.balboapress.com.au
1-(877) 407-4847

ISBN: 978-1-4525-1107-8 (sc)
ISBN: 978-1-4525-1108-5 (e)

Because of the dynamic nature of the Internet, any web addresses or links contained in this book may have changed since publication and may no longer be valid. The views expressed in this work are solely those of the author and do not necessarily reflect the views of the publisher, and the publisher hereby disclaims any responsibility for them.

The author of this book does not dispense medical advice or prescribe the use of any technique as a form of treatment for physical, emotional, or medical problems without the advice of a physician, either directly or indirectly. The intent of the author is only to offer information of a general nature to help you in your quest for emotional and spiritual well-being. In the event you use any of the information in this book for yourself, which is your constitutional right, the author and the publisher assume no responsibility for your actions.

Print information available on the last page.

Balboa Press rev. date: 02/12/2018

My parents with me when I was about six months old.

CONTENTS

INTRODUCTION

I HAVE WRITTEN THIS BOOK FOR three reasons:

(1) The feedback I was given on a Major Assignment for a Post. Grad. Diploma in Individual Psychotherapy & Relationship Therapy in which the lecturer wrote though I had spent time working on my role as a woman, my studies, my career, my ways of self expression and had achieved a great deal, I had not been able to lose the extra weight I wanted to lose. He suggested should I pay an equal amount of attention to the inside Helen who may still be a little girl who needs help to grow up and connect with my feelings of anger, shame, failure and loss of dreams then maybe the weight would come off and stay off.

(2) I gave my sister a copy of my assignment which was in book form and she lent it to her son who she told me said to her "To me she sounds very angry."

(3) The comments about my anger really surprised me as I had not been aware of feeling angry in my life so I decided to pay attention to the inside Helen by searching for the truth about my anger and my other feelings by writing a book.

As losing weight and keeping it off has been a life-long never ending battle I trust that by paying attention to the inside Helen I will connect with my feelings and find out the reasons I have a weight problem and let the weight come off and stay off—naturally and for good.

FOREWORD by Jim Gerondis

MY EXPERIENCE AS A STUDENT in Catholic schools was totally different from that of Helen's. Our parents were very friendly with three women of Irish descent, whom we called our Irish aunties. Because of their advice, my brother, two sisters and I received a Catholic education. I started at a pre-school run by nuns, then went to the Marist Brothers Primary School and High School at St Patrick's College run by Marist Fathers. We children were baptised in the Catholic church so we would not be different from the other children at the school.

When I was ten years old I came first in the class and I was given as my prize a Holy picture of Jesus wearing the Crown Of Thorns with a soulful look in His eyes and blood streaming down His face. This was my first concrete contact with the Catholic religion, symbolised by pain, suffering and torture which summed it up quite well.

My mother told us the Crucifixion was just a religious story not the truth—and not to believe anything we were told about it. She kept telling us emphatically all the religious stories we were being told were just stories and not the truth and we were not to believe any of them. I am glad I believed my mother completely.

The fact that my experience of going to Catholic schools was so completely different from that of Helen's I attribute to my mother's attitude.

My father was more religious than she was because he had spent three years as a youth in a Greek monastery where he was taught to read and write. He studied Greek Scripture while he was there with the monks.

My mother's view of religion was straightforward, simple and stated very clearly:-

"It's all rubbish" and I trusted and believed my mother rather than what I was told at school. My mother was ahead of her time—a liberated woman—independent and enterprising.

After my father died, she lied about her age and got herself a job she very much enjoyed in a chocolate factory.

She made many friends—had morning and afternoon tea and lunch breaks throughout the day and to her amazement was given a salary and two weeks paid annual holidays—all of which she had never before experienced in her whole life.

She was pleased, very appreciative and grateful she lived in a country like New Zealand where she had lived since she was married at the age of eighteen.

PREFACE

It may appear to anyone reading this book that I am anti-religion and anti-Catholic and an Atheist.

I consider myself to be an Agnostic.

I am interested in what every religion and science says about how the world and everything in it has come into existence.

When I looked at the "Inside Helen "and connected with why I am so angry I found the strongest and most enduring cause of my anger was my being told by a nun at school the story of Adam and Eve as the truth when I was nine years old.

I am angry about that and what I feel is even worse is that the existence of Genesis 1 was not mentioned at all.

I know that many people believe in the truth of the Bible and being Christian gives them both hope and comfort.

I believe in the right of Freedom of Religion.

I do not believe it is the right of any religion to assert what it believes to be true is the only truth which must be accepted by everyone on faith—in spite of lack of evidence to support its view—and even in spite of evidence against it.

By my making the Genesis 1 version more widely known I trust that more people will question:

(1) The teaching to children by Christian churches of the Adam and Eve Genesis 2 story as the literal truth without mentioning the existence of Genesis 1;

(2) The legitimacy of the attitudes which belief in the literal truth of Genesis 2—and not acknowledging the existence of Genesis 1—has engendered in both men and women over the centuries; and

(3) The ethos and the attitudes particularly of the Catholic Church and whether they need to be reviewed and revised in order to bring the church into harmony with the reality of life in the twenty first century.

ACKNOWLEDGEMENTS

I THANK OUR FIRST SON Denny and his partner Ann for the interest and support they gave me by reading the early drafts, their valuable suggestions and their encouragement to keep writing—all of which I appreciate very much.

In addition Ann edited most of my drafts in spite of her having limited time at her disposal and Denny did several final spell checks.

They both gave me a lifeline as no matter how many times I checked the typing there were mistakes and I was coming to the end of my tether.

I feel very grateful and very much indebted to both of them and especially to Ann.

My thanks and appreciation to our second son Michael for his diligent and blood-pressure raising (to both him and to me) input into my computer on numerous occasions.

He brought the book to life even though he agrees with his father that the whole enterprise is a complete waste of time because nobody is going to read it.

His help was willingly given most of the time and was both invaluable and indispensable.

Without his assistance I could not have overcome the hurdles along the way.

I am very grateful to our number three son Adam who when I said about five years ago that I was angry everyone else had an Email address and I didn't have one said to me it was not a problem and he would take care of it for me.

Within twenty four hours he had not only bought me a computer he had installed it and had connected me to the Internet. He provided me with my own Email address and showed me how to send and receive emails and how to use the Internet.

I appreciate and am very grateful to him for opening up a new world to me so willingly and patiently.

I thank my husband Jim for giving me the space and the time I needed to be able to do my own thing as he has done from the beginning of our association with each other. I had plenty of time to type on my computer while he watched every game of Rugby in which the All Blacks were playing over the three years I have been struggling with writing.

During this time my regard for anyone who has written a book and has had it published has increased a hundredfold.

I appreciate the feedback on my major assignment "Differentiation of Self" the lecturer gave me as without it I would not have been motivated to connect with my feelings by writing this book.

I am also grateful to the good psychologist whose report pointed me in the direction in which to proceed in my search for the truth.

1

SCHOOL

Because my father was born in Greek Thrace in Turkey and my mother was born in Athens Greece I have always felt different. I must look different too because I was and am often asked "Where do you come from?"

I didn't and don't feel Greek and I didn't and do not feel Australian even though I was born and grew up in Sydney.

One of my friends lived in Greece for two years as a child. He told me "when I was in Greece I was always called 'the Australian' and when I am in Australia I am always called 'the Greek.'"

Having to live in and adapt to two different cultures at the same time is not easy.

In the Greek Culture the first child was expected to be a male. Until I learned later that the sex of the child was determined by the father I felt guilty I had not been born a boy. I felt my father had never forgiven me for being born female and I am angry that he seemed to blame me for what was caused by him and not by me. I believe tension between first born girls and their mothers of which I am aware is caused unconsciously by this expectation.

When I was growing up it was quite common for marriages to be arranged between Greek families. We Greek Australian girls were not permitted to have boyfriends like the "immoral" Australian girls. We were only allowed to party at the home of friends of the family or attend Greek Community functions. We were not allowed or go out at night except in a group. Both sons and daughters were expected to live at home with their family of origin until they married a person of Greek background who met with their family's approval.

Life for young people became easier and more interesting when the "Olympic Club" (a Sports and Social Greek Youth Club) was formed. It was threatened with closure however after a boy and girl were seen kissing on the upper deck of the Showboat during our First Annual Ball.

My parents had taken me to Greece when I was eighteen months old until I was three and on our return we lived in a flat in Bondi and later in a rented bungalow opposite the beach near Bondi Public School.

I was taken out of that school after only being there for one term.

As a Non-Catholic attending a Catholic Convent School I suffered a huge culture shock.

I had never before my first day at school seen nuns dressed in black habits which covered them from head to toe except for their faces and hands.

I had not seen holy pictures of Jesus, one wearing a Crown of Thorns with blood dripping down his face and another of Jesus of the Sacred Heart with His Heart dripping drops of blood in the area of his chest.

I had never seen a figure of Jesus nailed to the cross, as was on the wall in every classroom. I was never told before, Jesus was crucified to save us from sin as we were all born with Original Sin and were I to die after having committed a mortal sin I would burn in hell for all eternity and in any case—**only Catholics were allowed into Heaven.**

For the first two years of school it was co-ed. The boys and girls were not allowed to talk together or use the same part of the playground which was divided by a rope into the girls' playground and the boys' playground.

I still feel guilty because I had talked with one of the boys at playtime and the nun in charge made him wear a frilly apron with a pink dummy pinned on it before she sent him out to play. On another occasion I was sitting on one of the benches when one of the boys sat beside me to show me a toy car engine which he was winding up and letting it unwind.

I asked him if he wanted me to put it on his head to see what would happen. He agreed and it didn't roll off his head as I had expected. It kept on entangling his hair so that he had to be taken down the street to the barber to have it removed. When this incident was announced in assembly I felt humiliated and shamed.

My parents had to pay fees and get special permission for me as a Non-Catholic to attend the Catholic school they had chosen on the recommendation of a family friend because of the "good discipline" maintained there.

I do not remember how I got to school on my first day. I felt very alone and very small and the school seemed so huge and unfriendly. I felt unwelcome, unwanted and alienated. I found out later I was the only non-Catholic overweight child of Greek descent in the whole school. I am still not sure that the perceived benefits of attending a private religious school were in fact greater than the enduring psychological harm I feel I have been and am still trying to understand and overcome.

Almost the whole time I attended that school from kindergarten till the end of high school I was unhappy and I am angry about that. I was in a constant state of anxiety in case I broke any of the rules or annoyed any of the nuns as I did when I made the sign of the cross, the Greek Orthodox way, using three fingers instead of using four fingers (as was the Catholic way) and one of the nuns came over and hit my hand with a ruler.

In second class I used to feel very frightened when the teacher (who was short and thin with a straight top lip) used to stand behind one of the boys and angrily thump him on both his shoulders at the same time because she was teaching us to write and he could not hold the pencil in the way she wanted him to do.

In High School I used to hide behind the girl sitting in front of me so the teacher wouldn't ask me a question, criticize and make fun of me the way she did to some of the other girls especially to a friend of mine whose father was not a Catholic. The only girls who were my friends were the ones who were only half Catholic and I felt some of them were discriminated against by the nuns and I felt personally traumatised by this.

The most lasting trauma I remember occurred in primary school in fourth class.

A nun who was not one of our teachers came into our classroom especially to tell us how God had created the world and us.

She told us that after God had created the world, He took dust from the ground and He made Adam. So Adam would not be lonely God took one of his ribs from which he created Eve to be his companion in Paradise.

God told them they must not eat from a certain tree—the Tree of Knowledge.

They disobeyed God because Eve had been tempted by the devil and gave Adam an apple from the tree to eat.

God was very angry and banished them from Paradise.

Because of Eve's sin she brought death and suffering into the world and because we were female we had to share her guilt forever.

I believed every word the nun had told us was the truth.

I felt shocked. I felt belittled as a human being. I felt ashamed to be female.

I felt the nun had placed a load of guilt on me I could not escape for all eternity.

My sense of self esteem, my self worth, my self respect and my confidence in women were all shattered.

I am angry I was told and believed a woman had caused such harm and being female I was also responsible for causing death and suffering in the world.

Because of the creation by God of Eve from one of Adam's ribs and what Eve had done, all women were tarnished. All women were born evil and inferior to all men.

All humanity had to suffer and die because of what Eve had done so women were to blame for all the pain and suffering in the world.

These negative feelings stayed with me for years after I had left school until a friend gave one of the children a little black leather bound copy of the Collins King James Holy Bible as a christening present. I opened it at the first chapter to verify the Adam and Eve story I had been told at school.

I was astonished to see not the story of Adam and Eve as I had expected, but a completely different version of the creation preceding it in Genesis 1.

I was not only astonished, I felt cheated I had not been told this story at the same time as I had been told about Adam and Eve so I had a choice as to which version, if either, I wished to accept.

I could hardly believe my eyes!

Here was a completely different account of the Creation!—a positive account—in which men and women were equal and there was no blame, disobedience, shame, guilt, anger and punishment from God—as was the case in the Genesis 2.

Here in Genesis 1 was a story of the Creation in which God was not a male God but male and female as it says in V26 God said "Let us make man in *our* image, after *our* likeness;"

V27 says "So God created man in his own image, in the image of God he created him, *male and female created he them.*"

I did not know at the time I was looking at the Protestant Bible and the Catholics have their own Bible.

By looking at the Catholic Bible on line I found, though a few words differ, what is said about the creation in the Catholic Bible is exactly the same as what is said in the King James Bible.

THE FIRST BOOK OF MOSES CALLED GENESIS

Chapter 1

1 The creation of heaven and earth, 3 of the light, 6 of the firmament, 9 of the earth separated from the waters, 11 and made fruitful, 14 of the sun, moon, and stars, 20 of fish and fowl, 24 of beasts and cattle 26 of man in the image of God 29 The appointment of food.

In the beginning God created the heaven and the earth.

2 And the earth was without form, and void; and darkness was upon the face of the deep. And the Spirit of God moved upon the face of the waters.

3 And God said, Let there be light: and there was light.

4 And God saw the light, that it was good: and God divided the light from the darkness.

5 And God called the light Day, and the darkness he called Night. And the evening and the morning were the first day.

6 And God said, Let there be a firmament in the midst of the waters, and let it divide the waters from the waters.

7 And God made the firmament, and divided the waters which were under the firmament from the waters which were above the firmament: and it was so.

8 And God called the firmament Heaven. And the evening and the morning were the second day.

9 And God said, Let the waters under the heaven be gathered together unto one place, and let the dry land appear: and it was so.

10 And God called the dry land Earth: and the gathering together of the waters called he Seas: and God saw that it was good.

11 And God said, Let the earth bring forth grass, the herb yielding seed, and the fruit tree yielding fruit after his kind, whose seed is in itself, upon the earth: and it was so.

12 And the earth brought forth grass, and herb yielding seed after his kind, and the tree yielding fruit, whose seed was in itself, after his kind: and God saw that it was good.

13 And the evening and the morning were the third day.

14 And God said, Let there be lights in the firmament of the heaven to divide the day from the night: and let them be for signs, and for seasons, and for days, and years.

15 And let them be for lights in the firmament of the heaven to give light upon the earth: and it was so.

16 And God made two great lights: the greater light to rule the day, and the lesser light to rule the night: he made the stars also.

17 God set them in the firmament of the heaven to give light upon the earth.

18 And to rule over the day and over the night, and to divide the light from the darkness: and God saw that it was good.

19 And the evening and the morning were the fourth day.

20 And God said, Let the waters bring forth abundantly the moving creatures that hath life and fowl that fly above the earth in the open firmament of heaven.

21 And God created great whales, and every living creature that moveth, which the waters brought forth abundantly after their kind, and every winged fowl after his kind: and God saw that it was good.

22 And God blessed them, saying, Be fruitful, and multiply, and fill the waters in the seas, and let fowl multiply in the earth.

23 And the evening and the morning were the fifth day.

24 And God said, Let the earth bring forth the living creature after his kind, cattle, and every creeping thing, and beast of the earth after his kind: and it was so.

25 And God made the beast of the earth, after his kind, and cattle after their kind, and every thing that creepeth upon the earth after his kind: and God saw that it was good.

26 And God said, Let us make man in our image, after our likeness; and let them have dominion over the fish of the sea, and over

the fowl of the air, and over the cattle, and over all the earth, and over every creeping thing that creepeth upon the earth.

27 So God created man in his own image, in the image of God he created him; male and female created he them.

28 And God blessed them, and God said unto them, Be fruitful, and multiply, and replenish the earth, and subdue it: and have dominion over the fish of sea, and over the birds of the air, and over every living thing that moveth upon the earth.

29 And God said, Behold, I have given you every herb bearing seed, which is upon the face of all the Earth, and every tree, in the which is the fruit of a tree yielding seed; to you it shall be for meat.

30 And to every beast of the earth, and to every fowl of the air, and to every thing that creepeth upon the earth, wherein there is life, I have given every green herb for meat: and it was so.

31 And God saw every thing that he had made, and, behold, it was very good, And the evening and the morning were the sixth day.

I felt very happy, relieved and thankful when I read this version of the creation.

Whoever had written the Bible were said to have been inspired by God so Genesis 1 was also inspired by God and was of equal authority to the Genesis 2 version we had been told at school.

I wondered why there were two versions of the creation in The Bible?

Theologian Bruce Vauter in the Introduction to his book Path through Genesis (Sheed and Ward. London. 1957) says the Semitic Historical Method is different from that of the Anglo-Saxon in that it consisted in laying parallel versions of the same story side by side, often repeating the same thoughts and expressions in each version, even though they may conflict. He says that although Genesis is a historical book not everything in it is history as the content was influenced by the time in which it was written and it consisted of what the authors wanted to teach us. Under the Law of Moses a woman was considered to be the chattel of her father and then of her husband, at least in theory.

Gentiles accepted that women were inferior in position and justified this because of the fact that women were the source of all evil and suffering.

In The Exclusion of Women from the Priesthood: Divine Law or Sex Discrimination? (Scarecrow Press Inc., Metuchen., N.J., USA., 1976) Ida Raming says that the Genesis 1 version of the Creation occurred later in time than that of Genesis 2 version. She says it reflects a further stage of development regarding the origin and the equality of the sexes. She also points out that Jesus says nothing whatever about woman having been derived from a man or that women are naturally inferior to men.

He regarded women as equal persons having equal rights and He specifically disapproved of the husband's one-sided right of divorce and any derived, inferior existence of women.

Edmund Leach in Genesis as Myth and Other Essays (Jonathan Cape London. 1969) asserts that all human societies have myths which express a reality which could not have been observed, in terms of phenomena which can be observed.

In the story of Adam and Eve, the reality of what could not be observed was the coming into existence of human beings and the phenomena which could be observed was the coming into existence of pots made out of clay.

This explains to me why people at that time believed a supernatural being had created man out of the dust of the ground.

The author says that myths are accepted not by reason but on faith—as being messages from God and it is common to find all important stories occur in several versions in all mythological systems.

I discovered these authors while reading for the Women's Studies Course and they provided answers which to me were and are persuasive and convincing.

I wonder why it is that though both stories of the creation are myths the Adam and Eve story is constantly referred to as the truth while Genesis 1 seems to be completely ignored by people who believe in the truth of the Bible.

Maybe the status of women in western society does not rest entirely on the Adam and Eve story however the belief that Genesis 2 is the literal truth has had a profound influence on how women were treated in the past and in how they are treated even now.

Eva Figes says in her book Patriarchal Attitudes (Virago, London 1978) that it is not in the interest of men to question the position of men and women in society and the norms of how they relate to each other. There is no motivation for them to do so because they have nothing to gain and would stand to lose not only their economic and social advantages but even more importantly, their precious sense of their own worth and superiority which bolsters their ego and how they regard themselves both in their public and in their private lives.

Assuming Eva Figes is right I am able to understand why most men, including my husband and our second son are not at all interested in the existence of Genesis 1 or in questioning the authority and truth of the Adam and Eve story.

What I can't understand is why feminists appear not to have loudly proclaimed the existence of Genesis 1 in the Bible in support of their claim for the inherent equality of both sexes.

If this is indeed the case why haven't they?

Is it because they had accepted what they were told as children about Adam and Eve and had no reason to check the authenticity of what they were told?

I am angry at the seemingly general acceptance of Adam and Eve as the truth especially after having read what is said by Arnold Whittick in Woman into Citizen (Athenaeum with Frederick Muller, London 1979) (P26).

The author says that up until the fourteenth century women in Italy enjoyed personal freedom and opportunities to study at the universities where they achieved renown for their intelligence and achievements. In 1377 however, the University of Bologna issued a decree stating that because woman is evil, the tool of the devil and the cause of man's expulsion from paradise, anyone who allows a women to attend college shall be severely punished. All association with women was expressly forbidden and women always had to be avoided. Whittick goes on to say that because of this decree not only the University of Bologna was closed to women but the theory that women were responsible for all the sin in the world then closed to them all the Italian and Spanish Universities as well.

He said because of this belief about women, generations of intelligent and talented women were condemned to live and die in ignorance and darkness.

He further states this attitude of men towards women that because of the temptations they provided for men they were a major source of evil and therefore had to be kept in subjection persisted well into the twentieth century.

It seems to me this attitude towards women at least as far as the Catholic and some other churches and cultures in the world are concerned is persisting into the twenty first century. In spite of all the progress towards equality in education and the status of women made since the decree was issued in the fourteenth century some beliefs and actions are still based on the literal truth of the story of Adam and Eve as they were seven hundred years ago!

Fortunately not all Catholics are still living in the dark past.

In an article in the Sydney Morning Herald on November 25th 1999 Chris McGillion (the Religious Affairs Editor) refers to a report commissioned by the Australian Catholic Bishops' Conference in which it was stated that a clear message received as the result of research was that the present culture of the church contained lack of respect for women leading to their subservient role and this had to be changed so men and women were treated as equal in order that women and children not be subjected to sexual victimisation in the Catholic church. The report states that it probably is the all male priesthood enshrined with power, position and superiority that is the part of the culture of the church which creates the conditions in which sexual offences against vulnerable people can more readily occur. How can this cultural attitude ever change when the Adam and Eve story continues to be taught as the literal Truth by the Catholic and other Christian churches?

In the S.M. Herald 19th May 2011, Saffron Howden quotes the Police Commissioner as saying that child abuse by fathers and stepfathers is under reported by up to ninety percent.

Many men are still taught as boys that God created man in His image and then created a woman not as an individual in her own right but as a companion for the man who was to rule over her because of her disobedience. Why would these men not feel they have the God-given right to use women even their own daughters or step daughters for their own sexual needs or gratification without regarding what they are doing as child abuse or sexual molestation?

Had they been taught as children the Genesis 1 version of the creation surely their resulting behaviour would be different?

I am angry that until recently the Vatican has been covering up and not reporting to the police the sexual abuse by priests of women and children.

The extent of abuse is still being uncovered, reported to the police and investigated.

The accused priests were moved to other parishes and continued to work as priests thus protecting the Catholic church but not other potential victims.

The Catholic Church has already paid out millions of dollars in compensation and is still paying compensation to victims of abuse by priests for offences committed and covered up over many years in many countries including Australia where there is evidence the church is still covering up sexual abuse of children by priests.

According to the first part of a report in The Sun-Herald, December 18, 2011 headed:

Dutch Child Abuse from The Hague:

Thousands of children had been sexually abused in Dutch Catholic Institutions and nothing was done by church officials to investigate the abuse or to help the victims according to a long awaited report by an independent commission because they were afraid of the scandals.

The Catholic church seems to put the good reputation of the church above the welfare of the children in their care.

Is the church only motivated by fear of scandals or is it also motivated by fear that there must be something inherently wrong with its belief system for these offences to be occurring?

In the SMH Weekend Edition July 17-18 2010, Barney Swartz in his article headed "Women priests join abusers on Vatican list of evils" said the Vatican had listed as a grave crime in the same category as paedophilia in the priesthood, the attempted ordination of women. Both these "grave crimes" listed by the papal government it was reported, warranted excommunication.

Why in 2010 did the Vatican consider the attempted ordination of women to be a "grave crime" warranting excommunication?

Could it be the men in the Vatican still believe all women are "Eves" and the source of all evil? or could it be they are unwilling to share their power and position with women? or both?

At the funeral held at a Greek Orthodox Church in the year 2010 the English translation of various "Tones" was printed in the booklet of the funeral service which was conducted in both Greek and English.

Part of the Translation of one of the Tones addressed God directly and told God in the beginning He had created and fashioned man in His own image and likeness and gave him a home in Paradise and made him the chief of His creation. When man because of the devil's influence was persuaded to eat the forbidden fruit and broke His Commandments man was sentenced to go back to the earth from which he had been made and we pray O lord You give him rest.

How sad the speaker feels when he thinks about death and sees the beauty which was once made in the image of God now lying in the graves devoid of grace and nobleness.

What is the mystery concerning humans and why were we given up to decay?

In truth, it is written that these things came to pass by ordinance from God who now gives her rest. Glory to the Father, the Son and the Holy Spirit.

I am angry that in the year 2010 the Genesis 2 version of the Creation and its consequences said to have come to pass by ordinance of a male God was read at the funeral of a woman who was my friend. I feel this was inappropriate in the twenty first century and not only an insult to her but to all those present.

I am not only angry about her funeral. I am angry about the manner of her death.

When she was diagnosed with terminal cancer she told me she did not wish to have any treatment and wished she could go to sleep and not wake up. When she told her doctor she wanted to be allowed to die as painlessly and as quickly as possible without treatment she told me her doctor said it may take time for her to die and she would suffer if she did not have treatment. She had her breast removed and her lymph glands removed before having Chemotherapy. The removal of her lymph glands resulted in the loss of the use of her right arm which she told me was worse than her having cancer. The chemotherapy caused the loss of her hair, the loss of her looks and loss of her quality of life.

I am angry that as she was terminally ill she was denied the humane right to die in the manner and the time of her own choosing.

2

MY EATING PROBLEM

When I did Women's Studies at the University of New South Wales for a Master of Arts Degree I was given information which caused me to question everything I had been told about God and the natural roles of men and women.

I'm angry I was not given any of this information when I was at school.

It was only when I later did the Post Graduate Diploma in Individual Psychotherapy & Relationship Therapy in Sydney that I realised how much my genetic make-up, the school I attended, the physical and emotional environment at that school and at home, my parents and the type of parenting they were able to give me, my position in the family and my Greek background influenced the choices I was able to make about the world and how I was able to fit into it and what kind of person I became.

I can tell from photos when my "eating problem" started. In all the photos up till my sister was born I appeared to be about average in weight.

We were at that time living in a small flat in Bondi after returning from living for eighteen months in Greece. My mother had hoped that we would stay in Greece however she was the one who most wanted to return to Australia. We returned to Sydney in time for my third birthday and my mother was six months pregnant with my sister.

A fortune teller in Greece had told my mother she would have another girl so she was not disappointed when my sister was born.

Because they had then been expecting a boy as their first child both my parents, especially my mother, were very disappointed they had had a girl when I was born. I am angry that in the Greek community at that time you were only really blessed as parents if you had a son. My mother told me she was so glad to have a baby of her own, she soon forgot about her initial disappointment. I did not forget however. I "remember" my birth and my mother's crying and turning away from me. Every year I feel angry and sad on my birthday and I have never celebrated it.

Until I started looking at the inside Helen and searching for the truth I believed the birth of my sister was the cause of my eating problem.

Through going on my inner journey and writing about it I found the birth of my sister was only one part of a series of different happenings at that time which caused me to use eating as a means of comforting myself and surviving in what felt like an uncaring world.

My sister was named after my mother's mother and looked like her side of the family while as was the custom at the time I was named after my father's mother. I looked like my father's side of the family all of whom looked more Jewish than Greek.

I had always felt as a child and until I was about eighteen years old that I had been adopted. When I discussed this with my cousin Katie she assured me this could not have been the case as it could not have been kept a secret and everybody would have known about it. I agreed with her and it changed how I felt in the present but did not change how I felt as a child.

Because I believed my sister was my mother's favourite I was astonished when she told me she too had not felt loved by either of our parents and she had felt no emotional connection with our mother who believed that cuddling, kissing or comforting a child was the wrong thing to do as it would spoil the child. The only time I can remember her touching me was when she smacked me. I can't remember either of my parents kissing or hugging me and felt surprised whenever I saw parents kissing or hugging their children in the movies.

When we lived in Greece an uncle used to keep touching me and poking his finger into my arm until I reacted by saying "Go way" and he would then laugh and do the same thing again and again. Everyone would laugh my mother told me.

I wonder why everyone Including my mother found teasing a little child so entertaining.

In our final year of the Counselling and Psychotherapy course we had to do and pass a major assignment on Differentiation of Self and in it I included some of my mother's story which she had told my sister's daughter Janet while she was living with them. What my mother said was recorded as she spoke and later transcribed.

The lecturer who not only taught at the college but was in private practice as a therapist—a university graduate and a published author— had given me three pages of feedback in which he included comments on the following part of what my mother had said:

"I don't really remember my father. He died when I was about four or five years old. There was a well on the property on which our new house was being built. My father wanted to go down the well to examine the water level so the men were lowering him down when they lost their grip and he fell to the bottom and was badly injured. He was rushed to hospital but died two weeks later. My mother was breast-feeding our baby sister at the time. The baby also died. The doctors told her the baby had been poisoned by her breast milk because of the stress she was under. The baby was given an emergency baptism and was christened Ismeni. Her body was placed at the feet of my father and they were both buried together.

My father's family lived in Kythera. His brother went rabbit shooting with a friend, who accidentally shot him dead. His other brother was a signalman on the railways in Ismir and was accidentally run over and killed by a train. My father had two sisters. One sister accidentally drank poison that had been stored in a soft drink bottle and died. The only member of the family who survived was his other sister who lived till she was 93 years old."

The lecturer wrote in his feedback he had particularly noted the incidence of early accidental death in my mother's father's family which must have had a strong influence which I did not explicitly acknowledge on my mother.

He said in families with such backgrounds there is often a strong underlying feeling of fear, secrecy and shame. My mother's fear of germs, her over-protection of us, her fear of other people and her closing down emotionally could all have been caused not only by the deaths in her father's family but by the devastating death of her own father. He said although she did not openly talk about her feeling of loss and grief she expressed these feelings in other ways. I appreciated his comments as he helped me understand my mother in a different way.

My mother's father (standing)

My mother (right) and her sister, after their father had
suddenly been taken away from them.

Belief in the power of The Evil Eye was very strong in Greece when my mother was growing up.

Unless a special ritual was carried out or a special prayer was said, a look of admiration, or envy from even a stranger could harm you or even cause you to die.

My father said this was "silly nonsense" however my mother knew the secret prayer (known to few) and used it for my sister and for me on more than one occasion when she believed we had been affected.

My own belief in the Evil Eye was aroused after I heard a nun at school say Angela in the Kindergarten class was "Too beautiful to live" and some time later we were told Angela had died and we were not told how or why she had died.

Neither of my parents had told me they were expecting another baby and had not prepared me for her birth. Once the baby was born my mother did not allow me to be involved with her in any way. I remember very clearly her saying to me in an angry voice in Greek "If you touch that baby I will cut off your hands."

I was very unhappy in this new situation and I tried to physically escape.

One of my earliest memories is of when I was just over three.

I was feeling very happy sitting in a toy car in the back garden of a neighbour. I was alone and enjoying the feeling of freedom. After some time a tall man wearing dark blue clothes came into the garden. I sensed he was a kind man and he seemed happy to see me. I was not worried when he lifted me up out of the car and into his arms while he told me it was not a good idea to go off alone like that because my mother was very upset about it.

That is all I remember about this adventure.

The only other time I remember feeling happy and free as a child was when I was about ten years old. I was on a very long beach with my sister and two younger cousins collecting shells in a bag while our parents walked behind us. Apparently we had gone too far ahead of our parents and my father suddenly came up and smacked me angrily, grabbed the bag of shells and threw it out to the sea. I felt shocked, upset and angry however this did not take away the feeling of happiness and freedom I had before he caught up with us.

As my mother had only spoken in Greek to me I could not speak or understand English when I went to Bondi Beach public school six months before I turned five.

What I remember most is enjoying watching the boys and girls noisily running around the playground having fun. I did not want to leave that school or our warm sunny house which I loved and in which my mother seemed to be so happy.

Our doctor told our parents to move inland as my sister had developed chronic bronchitis. On our last day I remember sitting alone on a sunny part of the carpet in the totally empty lounge room except for a built-in cupboard in which I had kept my toys and feeling both sad and angry. I wonder how our lives would have been had we not had to move from Bondi?

My father had bought a block of land near Centennial Park and because his solicitor had not informed him there was a restriction on the land as to how far forward the house could be built we ended up living in a two storey unfriendly cold dark isolated house which only my father liked probably because he spent much less time in it than we did.

I am sad we had to move from a one storey warm sunny house near the shops, the school and the beach to a large cold dark unfriendly two story house which I always felt was better suited to housing books than people as to me it looked and felt more like a library than a home. I was unhappy and I did not realise at the time how unhappy my mother must have been as she was unable to drive a car and could not walk to the shops to do her own shopping or walk me to school as she used to do.

I often watched as the new house was being built and I remember climbing over bricks and chatting with some of the workmen. When the polished wooden bannister on the staircase was finished, I bit into the wooden top which felt like I was biting the end of my pencil and quite enjoyable while I walked down the stairs.

When my father asked me about the marks I told him I had accidentally scraped the bannister with my bangle and he seemed to believe me and I felt very guilty.

It was not only the house I didn't like. I sensed my mother was unhappy too. I didn't like the fact that she was kept so busy looking after the house she seemed to have no time left to pay any attention to my sister and me.

She blamed having to go up and down the steps so many times a day for her miscarriage at five months of a male foetus followed later by giving birth to a stillborn baby girl. It was a very stressful time for my mother and for all of us.

I remember praying every night that someone would leave a baby on our door step.

It was around this time my mother's sister, husband and two children and her mother came from Greece and stayed with us till they bought a house of their own.

My grandmother died of cancer three months after their arrival.

I was not told she was very ill and I was not told when she had died.

I secretly watched from an upstairs window while her body was put into the ambulance.

None of her grand children was allowed to go to her funeral.

I remember having to be dragged away from her while I was crying and screaming when we were leaving Greece to come back to Australia.

She was not here long enough before she died for us to renew the bond we had in Greece. The one time I was allowed to see her while she was ill I remember her beckoning me into her room by saying in Greek "Come here my little star" (Astraki mou) which she called me ever since we lived with her in Greece because she said I lit up her life.

I felt as her first grandchild I was special to her and I felt she was very special to me.

Shortly after she had died her younger daughter's five year old son became very ill with rheumatic fever about a week or so after he had started going to school.

He was given my room and I was moved to the spare room downstairs and I felt upset as I had not been told why this was necessary. No child was allowed upstairs for several weeks. One day when the mothers were out I went up to see him and was shocked by how different he looked as his hair had grown very long.

As he was the only boy he was always given special attention not only from his mother but from our mother as well.

WITH MY GRANDMOTHER ON HER PATIO IN ATHENS

The evidence from photos shows a big increase in my weight after our relatives had arrived. When my aunt told me my mother had been giving me adult helpings when I was a child I realised I had always felt I had to eat to please my mother.

The feeling that as long as I keep eating I will be alright stayed with me for a very long time. My mother said she was told when I was a baby she had to feed me every four hours, ten minutes on each breast whether I was hungry before or after the four hours.

I do not remember ever feeling physically hungry or ever feeling satisfied after having eaten. I respond to external cues and eat food because it is there not because I am actually hungry. I can't tell when I am physically hungry or when I have had enough to eat as food does not satisfy me. I eat for emotional reasons to relieve my stress at feeling anxious or bored.

It was only when I was eating cake or chocolate or ice cream forbidden by my mother that I felt happier and more confident and the anxiety seemed to go away.

I am angry that when my mother asked our doctor for advice about my weight he just said to her "Don't give her any pocket money."

When I was unable to buy lollies after school as soon as I got home I would eat half a loaf of warm white bread recently delivered with butter and raspberry jam.

My mother would either be out or upstairs using her sewing machine.

My sister used to go next door as there was a girl her own age and a younger boy there with whom she could play. I stayed home and enjoyed myself with food instead of company.

I had my own key so I suppose I was a "latch key kid" and when I did not have my key I used to climb in through the kitchen window into a cold dark house which was quite scary. I am aware now that any major change or loss can cause depression and changes in eating behaviour in adults and also in children.

None of the adults in my life seemed to know I could have been depressed or to care.

I am angry nobody including our family doctor knew or cared that I needed help.

I feel sad that had anyone intervened when I was a child of four or five I may not have weighed eleven stone (70kg) when I was a child of eleven or looked like a middle-aged woman from the age of seventeen when I had finished school.

It was during the last two years at school that I had put on most of the weight.

When I was sixteen my mother took me to a biochemist who gave me a breathing test for my thyroid function which I remember was minus thirteen.

He put me on a diet of one thousand calories a day and told me to see him again in a month. I stayed on the diet for a month and I did lose weight.

However I did not stay on the diet and then I put on more weight than I had originally lost.

I am angry about this whole incident because I know now it started me on the yo yo dieting and eventual eating disorder which has ever since blighted and constrained my life.

In the last year of primary school even though I was never happy going to that school I was more stressed and even more unhappy.

I dreaded going to school every morning.

On my 3rd birthday with my mother
and God mother.

Photo taken on roof patio of the flats in which
we lived in Bondi when my sister was born.

With my cousins and my sister on Bondi Beach.

Almost every morning two or three boys in school uniform were there when I got off the tram. They used to call out "Fatty Finn the biscuit tin." and throw stones at me. I did not tell anyone about it at the time as I felt too ashamed and I feel uncomfortable writing about it now. I do not remember for how long this happened.

What I do clearly remember is how relieved I felt when after the Christmas holidays the boys were no longer there.

Though I was not interested in sport I would have liked to be able to play tennis in primary school and I was disappointed when I was not included in the tennis team. I am angry I was not encouraged to take part in any sport. On one occasion I entered and won the walking race.

The only thing that I liked about sports days was there were usually home made toffees in paper cups for sale. Sometimes my mother would give me money to buy one for me and one for my sister. I remember feeling very humiliated when my mother berated me in front of my aunt the day I had eaten the toffee I was supposed to have given to my sister.

When my mother was not at home when I got back from school which was usually the case I made my own toffees by melting sugar until it turned into caramel in the frying pan.

I had been happier at the Bondi Public School than I ever was at the private Catholic school. The attitude of the teachers, the boys and girls and the whole atmosphere of the school were all so very different. There were never children noisily running around having fun at the convent school. At the ring of a bell we had to line up in a row in front of the nun standing on the left side of the playground. When she rang the bell again we had to turn to the right and walk silently in line into class. If our classroom was upstairs, the prefects were there to make sure we did not talk or touch the handrail on the way up the stairs.

Some of the nuns told us stories about the saints.

I felt quite upset when a nun told us about the woman saint who used to whip herself on her back until she was bleeding to punish herself for not preventing herself from having evil thoughts. Girls who crossed their legs were told they "had made Our Lady blush" and we were told wearing shorts or sleeveless tops was not an appropriate way in which to dress. A priest used to visit us regularly and what I remember about those visits are the times he pointed to some of the girls and told them they looked like they would "make good nuns."

Towards the time of the Leaving Exam I was going to school seven days a week.

Every Saturday we did past Leaving Certificate Papers and every Sunday afternoon the girls who were doing music as one of the subjects for the Leaving Certificate had to perform in a concert for the nuns. I do not remember the concerts.

I remember that before every piano or singing exam my teacher would pin a Holy Relic on my uniform, bless herself and say a prayer. My music teacher had a round face and she was short and plump and kind and I liked her.

I loved music and I always did well in music exams.

Being good at Music seemed to be much less valued than being good at Sport.

I would have liked to continue having lessons with my music teacher after I left school.

As this was not allowed she referred me to a singing teacher at the Conservatorium of Music.

He was not only a singing teacher he was also a very well known opera singer and I liked going to my singing lessons and being accompanied by his pianist when I sang songs. After a year of singing lessons with him I Passed the Public Examinations and Obtained the distinction of Associate in Music. Singing (A.Mus.A)

I was pleased and happy about this however I did not tell my family or anyone else about it as I did not feel any of my extended family or friends would have been interested.

My mother used to tell me stories about things I used to do or say or what happened when I was three years old. One of these stories was that whenever she took me out if there was any music being played in the street she would have a hard time persuading me to leave and had to physically drag me away.

She told me whenever she tried to practise the piano with me on her lap, I would pull her hands away from the keyboard. And when her piano teacher used to sit me on her lap while she played the piano whenever she stopped playing I would pull her hands onto the keyboard Other stories she told me about how I behaved as child also gave me insight into who I am now and I loved hearing them.

There were no stories about me after my sister was born and there were no stories about what my sister did or said when she was little either and I wondered why. Looking back I feel moving house, having a miscarriage and then a still born baby and the death of her mother were all too much for her and she could only cope by her shutting down emotionally.

I can't remember ever seeing my mother happy once we had moved from Bondi Beach.

In the photo of me and my parents in the front of this book my mother looks sad to me and I assume it is because she failed to have a son as her first born. Though I know I did not choose to be a girl I feel I let her down because I was not born a boy.

Feeling I was to blame for my mother's unhappiness has stayed with me since childhood.

When I was in high school the girls started talking about their boyfriends. When I told my father this he said to me "You are too sensible to do that."

I did not like being different so I told the girls I also had a boyfriend.

My boyfriend was a framed photo of the man to whom one of my cousins was engaged.

I was thirteen and he was twenty three and I thought he looked very handsome in his graduation cap and gown. I kept his photo in my desk and I was very disappointed that none of the girls asked me if she could see it.

My teacher in sixth class had looked at me as she said "One of you girls is intelligent enough to top the class but is too lazy to do so."

I am angry not one of our teachers seemed to have considered it may have been inadequate teaching which caused my "laziness" instead of an inadequacy in me that prevented my doing well at school.

At the Twenty Fifth School Re-union which was the only one I attended most of our class were there and some of our high school teachers were there too. I did not recognise any of the nuns.

The heavy black serge robes had been replaced by lighter shorter gowns which exposed their ankles and their shoes. Their hair which was previously hidden behind a white starched band around their faces was now visible and they looked completely different from the nuns with whom I had spent eleven years of my life.

When one teacher said to me "Do you remember me?" I said "No" as she did not look like the teacher I did remember and feared.

She said "You did very well when you left school you wretch! I couldn't get you to do anything!"

My being at school which is supposed to be the happiest time of my life was for me joyless and very unhappy. The emphasis at our school was on obeying rules and religion.

We did not have a science lab and were not taught science as a subject.

I remember one teacher referring to the idea we may have evolved from monkeys as a joke—laughing and saying that some of us may have come further than others.

My feeling was that our school existed not to educate girls to take their place in the world.

My feeling was that our school existed in order to provide the Catholic Church with nuns.

Our nuns wore wedding rings as they were "married" to Jesus.

They had to take an Oath of Obedience and one of Poverty.

Any property they owned had to be given to the Church.

Had they not been taught that Genesis 2 was the truth and they had to suffer in this life to atone for Sin in the world so they could have everlasting life in heaven with Jesus when they died, would they have chosen to become nuns I wonder?

After I became aware of the existence of Genesis 1 and had later visited the Vatican, I felt nuns and priests had been manipulated and used by the Catholic church for its own ends.

I was shocked when I saw the door made of gold and all the other priceless treasures in the Vatican. I felt the church and all its teachings were organized not for the spiritual welfare of its followers but to satisfy the church's need for power and control over people's lives and in order to maintain and increase its material wealth, prestige and influence.

I felt cheap labour in the form of nuns and priests was part of the well organized plan by the church which seemed either to be indifferent to the extent of the personal suffering it inflicted on many of its followers or else rejoiced in their suffering as it would lead them to heaven.

Where does love come into the equation when a person is basically controlled by fear?

When I was at school my life was dominated by fear of God who knew everything I was thinking or doing. I was told and believed God was always watching me and would punish me if I did or even thought of doing anything wrong or against the rules.

Even eating meat on a Friday was a sin at that time. My husband told me when he was at school how he felt whenever he saw his parents breaking that rule. He agonised about the possibility of their going to hell for doing so.

I am angry the changes the Catholic church has made such as regarding the existence of hell and purgatory (which I have been told no longer exist) are of no benefit to me or to those of my generation who were subjected to the fear of eternal damnation.

These changes cannot undo the harm the direct and indirect messages based on the literal truth of Genesis 2 caused me and I believe are still causing me and many other people.

I have followed the advice of the good psychologist who in her report told me I had to undo and confront what I was taught was the truth in order to transcend it otherwise it would maintain its restricting power over me.

This is what I have been doing and continue to do by writing about the creation stories and the effect they had on me. I feel the most restricting thing I had to confront was Genesis 2.

I was unable to confront Genesis 2 until I discovered the existence of Genesis 1 which is the most important challenge to the truth of Genesis 2 right there in the Bible itself.

Only when the Catholic Church acknowledges the existence of Genesis 1 as a completely separate and a later more evolved account of the creation will the Vatican by changing the basis of its belief system, be able to change what it teaches, especially as regards the status and role of women. Only then will the whole ethos of the Catholic church be able to change and move into the twenty first century.

Among the stories my mother told me about myself as a three year old was the time she had asked the woman who was helping her with the housework to tidy the drawers in her room.

When I saw the helper take my mother's clothes out of her drawer I said to her "If you put them back, I will not tell my mother" she said.

I feel how I reacted shows even at that age I had a strong sense of justice which together with a love of music is still part of who I am.

I do not know what effect telling us Adam and Eve as fact had on the other girls in my class.

I remember very well the traumatic negative damaging effect it had on me.

That the Catholic and other Christian churches ignore Genesis 1 by treating it as part of Genesis 2, is to me inherently wrong because of the negative consequences, not only for how the women and children have been and are regarded and treated, but ultimately for the men.

I feel angry the Christian churches seem to be ignoring the existence of Genesis 1 in order to maintain their sense of male supremacy and if they have knowingly and deliberately made this choice, it seems to me to be reprehensible, unfair, unjust, unjustified and unjustifiable.

I am angry because I feel it is the church belief in the literal truth of Genesis 2 and basing all its teachings on this version of the creation—which has caused evil in the world, not woman!

Many Catholics are leaving the church and many priests and nuns are also challenging the teachings of the Catholic church and leaving it in order to get married.

In view of recent allegations, the subject of celibacy and whether it is in any way linked to the sexual abuse of women and children, needs to be researched by an independent task force.

ABC Four Corners on 2nd July 2012 in Sydney exposed sexual abuse by priests on boys which has resulted in two suicides and allegations of cover up by the church.

The then Prime Minister in November 2012 announced a wide—ranging Royal Commission into the sexual abuse of children in the church, government and not for profit institutions would take place throughout Australia and this was welcomed by most people including members of the opposition.

As far as the teaching of religion is concerned I agree with what journalist Peter Fitzsimons says in his article in the Sydney newspaper the Sun Herald on the 14th August 2011 under the heading—Religion has no place in Education.

In this article Peter Fitzsimons recounts that he went to kindergarten in 1966 and says his teacher taught them not only the three R's of reading, writing and arithmetic but as he attended a state school a fourth "R" which was Religion had to be included for one hour a week. During this time they had to study the Christian scripture stories as if they were facts. He says for one hour a week they had to learn as fact the story of how God made the world in six days and rested on the seventh and how all humans are born evil because Eve who had been made from Adam's rib was tricked by the devil in the guise of a snake which talked her into eating the forbidden fruit.

Peter Fitzsimons says he thinks it is outrageous that religion was part of his public education. He asks as a five year old how could he make a distinction between learning what were facts and what were only fiction. He says at that age of course he could not and it was not until he was fifteen years old and reading books by Bertrand Russell that he could free himself from those stories with which he had been indoctrinated as the truth.

He points out our whole system in Australia is predicated on separation of church and state which must take a neutral view about religion and not endorse or encourage teaching of any specific religion in state schools.

In his opinion there should be no teaching of religion in state schools.

I feel it is not fair to teach religious stories as the truth in any schools in Australia.

As religion has been and is important to human beings it is appropriate the schools teach religion but not in the way it was taught in 1966.

As Australia is becoming increasingly multi-cultural would it be appropriate for classes on Comparative Religion to replace scripture classes in state schools and even in private schools?

Recently the alternative to attending scripture classes in state schools has been attending ethics classes which are very popular. Before this children who did not attend the scripture or special religion class were not given any tuition during that time.

Ethics classes were on trial but they have now been put on the same footing as special religious classes by being able to fund themselves through tax deductible donations for the administration of their programs.

Even though Australia was founded as a Christian country would it be in the interest of all children in all schools not to be indoctrinated into any particular religion?

Would it be better for children to be able to make their own decision about what they believe is true when they become adults if they were to be taught about all the established religions and not just about christianity?

Would it be in the best interest of children and society as a whole if all schools were non-denominational and state schools were of such a good standard that the parents would no longer send their children to private schools and they would cease to exist?

3

EDUCATION

I REMEMBER THE ONLY TIME I raised my hand to answer a question at school I was in third class. At the beginning of the lesson one of the two nuns standing in front of the class said to us:

"Marconi invented the Wireless."

At the end of the lesson she asked the class "Who invented the wireless?"

Without hesitation I raised my hand and said "Marconi."

The nuns looked at each other and all the girls seemed to be looking at me and I felt myself blushing as I felt I had done something reprehensible.

It is now disputed as to who was the first person to invent the wireless.

The only thing I remember learning in primary school is probably incorrect!

I am angry that I had trouble with numbers and calculations while I was at school and still do.

In sixth class the girls in each row had to take part in weekly mental maths competitions.

My mind still goes blank and I freeze whenever I try to do any additions or subtractions without writing the numbers down and even then I find it difficult.

I remember the girls in the row which came last in the mental maths competition had to go to the front of the room, line up in front of the teacher's desk and hold out the palms of our hands for her to strike us with a thick wooden ruler. I felt outraged at the time this happened to me and I am still angry that it did. I suspect this is the reason I dislike and am unable to do anything involving numbers to this day.

We had only two teachers in the whole school who had qualified as teachers by going to university and they taught high school. I doubt that our maths teacher in sixth class had had any training as a teacher.

My sister went to the same school and she did not like being at that school either.

When she had finished the first year in high school, she enlisted the help of two older girl cousins who had attended a Church of England school to persuade father to allow her to leave the Catholic school and go to the same school the cousins had attended and liked.

By the time my mother and I had returned home my sister had been enrolled at the new school and had already bought her new uniform.

At no stage of my ordeal at the Catholic school had it ever occurred to me that I could change schools. I believed I had no choice but to stay there until the end of high school.

When I had completed first year of high school we moved to Katoomba for a year.

My father felt we would be safer away from Sydney during the war. He stayed in Sydney and only came up to Katoomba on the weekends.

The Catholic convent school I attended there was a year behind my school in Sydney so on my return to Sydney the following year the nun in charge said I would not be allowed to sit for the Intermediate exam at the end of the year unless I could catch up to the rest of the class. I enjoyed having to work hard to try to catch up. I not only caught up and was allowed to sit for the Intermediate exam I passed it with an A in Music and French and Bs in English, Latin, History, General Maths and Art.

Next year which was Fourth Year we were asked who in the class wanted to go to University. When I asked my mother she said "A university education is wasted on a girl. All you have to do is finish school, get married and have children."

I am angry neither my father nor any teacher at school intervened on my behalf.

I had done reasonably well in the Intermediate so I expected a teacher or my father to speak to my mother for me even though I had not openly or directly asked for their help.

When no help eventuated I felt I had to accept what my mother had said as final.

I was not aware of how angry I felt at that time. I just had a compulsion to eat forbidden food.

I ate cakes, chocolate and Ice cream until I had put on twenty kilos without knowing why.

No one seemed to notice what I was doing and no one seemed to care.

I dropped my matriculation subjects and passed the Leaving Certificate with the bare minimum of four B's which was a huge disappointment to my father.

He valued education and he had not supported me because he believed "There can only be one Captain on a ship" and care of the children was my mother's responsibility and not his.

I am angry I could not go to university like the Greek Australian boys were encouraged to do. I was only allowed to do the Sydney Kindergarten Teachers College Course because one of my cousins was already enrolled there. The college accepted my late enrolment after I sat and passed the IQ test.

I enjoyed the course which consisted of two years of lectures covering such subjects as psychology, music, art, sociology, anthropology and education and the last year working with the children at three different kindergartens.

At the end of third year I graduated and received my diploma at the Sydney Town Hall and both my parents especially my father seemed happy to be present.

I felt this course was of great benefit to me both at that time and especially later in my life when we had kindergarten age children of our own.

I am angry my sister Lilian who had matriculated and wanted to study physiotherapy was not allowed to go to university either. As we were not given any other choice she also graduated from the Kindergarten Teachers Training Course a couple of years after I had.

Things only changed for the better for me after I married and left home.

After we had our first child I successfully applied to study for the Leaving Certificate by Correspondence and often did my assignments cuddling the baby in my left arm while I was writing assignments with my right hand.

One of the best times in my life was seeing that I had passed when Jim drove me down to the Sydney Morning Herald building the night they published the results and posted them outside. I still have the Certificate from the New South Wales Department of Education which states that I "A Private Study Candidate obtained pass standard in the Leaving Certificate Examination in the following six subjects; English, French, Modern History, Ancient History, Economics and Theory and Practice of Music."

My mother was still opposed to my going to University and this time she could not stop me. Jim said to my father who on instructions from my mother had said to him "It is wrong for Helen to leave the children to go to lectures and you should stop her." that he knew how important it was for me to go to University and he fully supported my going to my lectures. I am angry about my mother's attitude and I am even angrier about the attitudes of her friends all of whom supported her.

It did not make sense to me it was alright for other mothers including themselves when their children were young to leave them with a baby sitter for two or three hours while they went shopping, had lunch or went to the hairdresser however it was not acceptable for me to leave my children with a minder for two or three hours while I went to university lectures.

Even though I had a driving licence I could not drive as I did not like driving as I felt too anxious. Jim did the shopping and the transporting of the children and gave me as much time to study as he could. At the time of my Final Exams he took all the children and stayed with his mother in Wellington until the exams were over.

It took me eight years to finish the five year course and I felt very fortunate and very glad we were able to have more babies during that time. I felt very grateful the doctor who looked after me was kind and supportive of my studying and also believed in natural childbirth.

When he thanked me for a Christmas card he added he was not a Christian. As I liked and admired him and the kind of person he was I decided I would not be a Christian either.

Jim, Mrs Smith who minded the children while I went to lectures, the children including our four weeks old baby and my parents were at Sydney University for my Graduation as Bachelor of Laws. As I was not able to practise because of my family commitments I continued to study and several years later Jim, our seven children and my mother were at my Graduation as a Master of Laws. This Graduation was not as exciting and happy as the Bachelor of Laws one had been as my father and Mrs Smith had both died in the meantime. Had it not been for "Miff" and Jim who was so capable and so willing to involve himself with the care of the children and household tasks especially cooking none of this could have happened. Most importantly it could not have happened if it were not for my mother-in-law.

I will always be very grateful to her for being the kind of mother she was to her children which enabled Jim to be a very involved father at a time when they were very rare.

I am angry not only because of the extra stress my mother caused me but because of the cost to him and our children none of whom deserved the stressed, irritable, impatient, over-reactive person with whom they had to live.

I was like a pressure cooker always having to let off steam by yelling in order to survive. One of our then neighbours said to me she hoped she would never yell at her children the way I yelled at mine.

A few years later she not only yelled at her children so did her husband who also included a few swear words. When I accidentally met her recently she recalled these incidents and added that they had had only three children!

By blaming my weight for all my problems I avoided coming to terms with the deep feelings of rejection I had at school and at home where I felt I had been displaced by my sister.

I was able to repress my need to go out on dates and have fun, buy attractive clothes, and enjoy music and dancing by eating. I craved forbidden food not knowing why I was unable to stop myself from eating it and gaining more weight against my conscious will.

As an adult I felt unable to satisfy any of these needs until I lost weight so I kept part of my of my life on hold by not doing what I wanted to do till I lost weight which I couldn't do so I felt I was trapped in a vicious cycle.

I joined Weight Watchers five times each time telling myself it would work this time and it didn't. I am angry it did not work for me and it worked for all the other people in the group. I finally acknowledged it would never work for me and I needed to find another solution.

Restricting what she allowed me to eat instead of letting me make my own choices, was my mother's way of dealing with my eating problem and it did not work either.

She did not make dessert unless guests were invited and she kept a supply of cakes, biscuits and chocolates in a locked cupboard in the kitchen. I had collected enough keys to enable me to have access to that cupboard whenever I wished and I felt glad rather than guilty about doing so when she was not at home.

My mother would not allow me to have dolls.

She told me the story of when I was three and she would not buy me the doll I wanted when we were out shopping and I started to cry. She said she did not know what else to do so she smacked me until a woman came up and said to her "If you don't stop hitting that child I will report you to the Child Welfare."

When our relatives arrived from Greece my uncle gave me a Dutch doll he had won in a raffle on the ship. I liked that doll which was wearing a cap and clogs and after a couple of days it disappeared. Later I heard my mother say to some of her friends "Helen never liked playing with dolls" when the truth was she did not allow me to have dolls with which I could play.

At school I had healthy food like rissoles and lettuce for lunch while the other girls had sandwiches and cakes.

I always ate my lunch on my own away from the other girls in my class and even now I prefer to eat alone.

As my mother was afraid of my catching germs she did not allow me to play with any other children except relatives until I went to school.

Even when I was a teenager she did not allow me to choose the food I wanted to eat or the clothes I wanted to wear.

I am angry I had to eat whatever she had cooked and had placed on the plate for me.

I am angry I could not fit into ready made clothes and I had to wear clothes my mother or her dressmaker had made and I had no control over what clothes I wore until I was married.

I was nine when my mother was in hospital having had a still born baby girl. At that time my father came into my room, sat on the edge of the bed and said "As I have no son, you are my son" I clearly remember those words and how sad and serious he looked when he said them.

I remember years later when I was seeing the psychotherapist in Wellington I recalled a dream in which I was nine years old and I lifted up a five year old boy and placed him on my shoulders. I feel I have been carrying that boy in the form of fat ever since.

I remember my mother saying to me many times: "You should have been a boy."

I liked the company of boys however I never consciously wanted to be a boy as far as I can remember. I longed to be the girl I felt I was not allowed to be.

During the counselling course which was an experiential personal growth course in which I had enrolled because in spite of having had professional help I had not overcome my eating problem I became more self aware and learned a lot more about myself.

By doing this course I was able to connect with my emotional needs for the first time and specifically my need to be loved and accepted by my father as the little girl I had been and as the woman I had become. As my father continued to believe and act as if I were his son, he was incapable of being the warm, tender, loving, caring and protective father I wanted and needed. Until I was doing that course I feel I had repressed those feelings.

My father often used to say "All women are stupid except Helen because she is like me."

I liked being treated as his intellectual equal however I felt emotionally deprived.

I kept all my pretty girly things including clothes in a suitcase in my wardrobe.

Every now and then I would take everything out of the suitcase to look at and hold every item then put everything back into the suitcase and hide it in the wardrobe again.

I guess I was avoiding my father's disapproval which he showed me by giving me an "ugly look" or by giving me "the silent treatment" which could sometimes last for weeks or even months. I was not aware of feeling frightened of him however I realise now I must have been at least on a subconscious level. Even though I was not then aware of Honour Killings my instincts told me how dangerous it would be for me if I were to have a real boyfriend.

My father had lived in Turkey where honour killings were culturally acceptable until he was fourteen years old and I believe this had a big influence on his attitude towards me and my sister and why he was so strict with us. On several occasions he hit me at the instigation of my mother who used to complain about me the minute he came home. Until I disposed of it, he used to hit both my sister and me with the whip he used while horse-riding in Centennial Park. I can't remember what I did with the whip. I was relieved and pleased it was never replaced.

My father was the youngest of a large family whose home and almost the whole village was destroyed by an Earthquake. His eldest brother who had lived in Australia for several years brought my father then fourteen years old to Sydney and later together with my father brought his mother and all the family to Australia.

My father loved living in Australia and never looked back.

He was energetic, enthusiastic, optimistic, present and future focused.

He did not speak of the past or of his childhood or of his life before he came to Australia other than telling us something about his family history.

He loved people and being with people and he was always willing to help anyone especially members of his extended family whenever they asked him for his help whether financial or otherwise.

He told us his father had been a notary and acted as the lawyer in the Greek village of Peristassi (now Turkish Sarkoi). His grandfather had been an architect who had designed the cathedral which had also been destroyed in the earthquake.

Other than his telling us he had worked twenty hours a day when he first came to Australia, my father did not tell us anything about his early experiences in Sydney.

His major contribution to his new country was his opening of the first real Milk Bar in Australia in Martin Place Sydney on the third of November 1932.

His success and interest in business had made life harder for our mother.

I am angry she had to look after us on her own even during the school holidays most of which we usually spent in Katoomba for the beneficial fresh air.

I can remember only one happy holiday and that was when my father came with us and we stayed at the hotel near the Railway at Katoomba and not at the usual guest house at which we stayed with our mother. Why it was so happy for me was my mother did not have to cook and the four of us all sat down together for meals.

Had my mother encouraged my father to be involved with us I feel he gladly would have been. I regret he was not and feel perhaps our mother had unconsciously deprived us of our father because she grew up without a father as he died when she was about four years old.

Perhaps it was not that but because at that time there were strictly defined sex roles to which most people adhered. Men were the providers and women looked after the home and family.

One only has to visit one of the shopping malls to see how much more fathers are involved with their children today. It is quite common now to see men on their own with a baby strapped to their chest or pushing a stroller or even caring for a baby and other children at the same time or whole families out shopping together.

It is now possible to see men with their children on public transport or walking on the street which would have been impossible years ago when men were not so involved with children. Sundays when we were children our father used to take us for a drive to La Perouse or Manly or to visit relatives in various suburbs. There was very little involvement with him on any other day of the week. One Sunday I accidentally caught a little fish in a rock pool at La Perouse by fishing with a bent pin on the end of a piece of string.

When I pulled up the string there was a little fish attached to it. I felt very upset and the fish was flapping and I was crying until my father managed to release it back into the water.

Our mother told us she wanted to be a teacher and there was no money for her education. I am very sad about this as I feel had she been a teacher not only she would have been more fulfilled and happier, all her family would have benefited and would have been happier too.

AN ANNIVERSARY OF THE OPENING OF THE
BLACK AND WHITE MILK BAR IN MARTIN PLACE
WHEN THE DAY'S TAKINGS WERE DONATED
ANNUALLY TO A DIFFERENT CHARITY, USUALLY
TO THE DALWOOD HOME FOR CHILDREN.

MY PARENTS WERE MARRIED IN THE
ST JAMES ANGLICAN CHURCH.

FATHER REFUSED TO HAVE ANYTHING MORE TO DO
WITH THE GREEK CHURCH AFTER RIVAL CHURCH
FIGHTING HAD DIVIDED THE GREEK COMMUNITY.

4

FINDING A PARTNER

ONE OF MY FIRST COUSINS was married to a young woman from Wellington New Zealand. My father had told me he would go to New Zealand with me for a holiday when I finished school. As he could not do so, he arranged for me to go with her by ship on a surprise visit home. Her parents, her brothers and sister were delighted to see her when they came to the wharf to meet me. The whole family was very hospitable, warm and kind especially the elder son whom I had met when he came to Sydney to visit his sister. His parents had told him to be sure to see my parents to thank them for accepting their daughter into the family. When I opened the front door one afternoon, there was this medium height man with brown hair, hazel eyes and wide shoulders wearing a tweed jacket with a blue paisley tie looking at me. He stood there and it took some time for him to tell me who he was and why he had come. When my mother asked him to dinner at which my lawyer friend from up the road was also present, everyone sat around the table and I had to serve each person a plate of Chicken Maryland which was my mother's specialty. We went through a similar ritual every night and I very strongly disliked this way of serving and eating food.

I was delighted to find when in Wellington that the whole family planned and prepared the food which was placed on the table in big platters from which we all helped ourselves to whatever we wanted.

What is more the whole family as well as having helped prepare dinner also cleaned up after dinner unlike what happened at our home where my mother did it all herself.

The elder brother Jim was studying to be a pharmacist and was apprenticed and worked in a pharmacy while he was attending the Pharmacy College. During his lunch break he would come home to have a chat with his sister Connie and me.

On the weekends he took us on drives around the Wellington harbour foreshore. He also drove us to the Botanical Gardens to see the magnificent display of beautiful tulips of different colours and up to Mt Victoria to admire the view.

Every night we would all have dinner together. It was always a joint effort and the whole atmosphere was warm, happy and relaxed and the opposite of what it was like in our home. Jim's mother had two boys and two girls and unlike all the other Greek mothers I knew, she treated them all equally and expected the boys and the girls to share in all the household tasks including cleaning floors, dusting and cooking.

One evening he took his sister, his brother and me to a Dinner Dance at The National Club.

I could tell he did not enjoy dancing as he was concentrating more on moving his hand up and down my back rather than moving his body in time to the music.

I did not understand why he was giving me so much attention and giving me presents.

He gave me a camera, a gold locket and went to a great deal of trouble and spent half of his week's wages to buy me a bottle of "Tabu" perfume—which was hard to get—because I had told him how much I liked it.

The day we were leaving he met me in the city to say goodbye and asked me to kiss him which I refused to do as the nuns had warned us that kissing a boy was a very serious matter not to be undertaken lightly.

I was not so attracted by how he looked or how he sounded.

What really attracted me was the smell of his body.

Years later a psychologist told me of an experiment in which a group of men were asked to put onto the floor in the middle of the room the singlets they had been wearing while exercising. An equal number of women were asked to select the singlet the smell of which most appealed to each of them.

After all the DNA had been analysed it was found that each of the women had chosen the singlet of the man whose DNA differed the most from that of her own. This was nature's way it was concluded of ensuring the greatest benefit to any children they may have together.

Until I was told of this research I had not realised that of any of the men who had shown an interest in me at that time he was the one my nose had decided I wanted to be the father of my children!

One year later when he went back to Wellington from Sydney he sent me a letter saying he would like me to help him to get to know my sister and his parents sent a letter to my parents asking for them to approve of him as a suitor for my sister.

I was very hurt and very angry. I thought he liked me so I felt shocked and annoyed it now seemed he was only being so attentive to me because he was interested in my sister!

I was also hurt and angry my parents did not consult me before replying to his parents that their younger daughter was unavailable however their elder daughter was available should they be interested in her. My father had been very eager to accept such an arrangement because he had warned me that unless I lost weight not only my lawyer friend but no man would ever want marry me. He had stopped the car on the way home in order to tell me this. Unfortunately his words had the opposite effect to the one he had hoped to achieve as I kept gaining weight not losing it.

I felt I had been rejected because I was too fat yet the more I tried to lose weight the more I gained weight and I could not understand why this was happening.

I was angry with Jim for not having the guts to approach my sister himself and I was angry with myself for not realising that he had just been using me as means of getting to know her.

After I thought about it for a while I realised he and my sister had more interests in common such as love of sports. They were more alike in body type and in colouring and looked more suited to each other and more like a couple than he and I did.

I felt I had more in common with his brother Dino who liked music and singing and was an excellent dancer. I liked accompanying him on the piano whenever we had a sing song. We were more alike in colouring and body type and perhaps we looked more like a couple than Jim and I did. I could not even imagine my being married to him however or asking Jim to help me to get to know him so I could marry him which is what Jim had asked me to do for him regarding my sister.

This whole incident made no sense to me and I was angry, unhappy and confused.

I felt that was the end of our relationship, however it wasn't. Although we had different interests and values, we had similar temperaments and backgrounds so there was an intrinsic affinity between us.

What I feel is most frustrating in our relationship is that rugby, golf and all sports, so loved by him are so boring, uninteresting and in some cases offensive to me.

He loves all sports especially rugby—and I dislike all sports—especially Rugby!

I feel this creates a permanent emotional distance between us and that is just how it is.

He is interested in horses and I am not. He listened to the horse races one holiday weekend and I had never heard horse races in our family home before. The sound to me was ugly, jarring and very unpleasant and I felt he was committing a mortal sin listening to the races in our home while my parents were away.

I felt and still feel we really live in different personal worlds and if it were not for pheromones I would most probably not have had anything to do with him.

He is a natural athlete. He excelled at football and in swimming which he loved and had taught himself. He excelled at soccer and when we moved to Sydney he excelled at golf.

At the University of Otago he was asked to be the captain and coach of their first soccer team, which was unbeaten for the season and out of one hundred goals he scored sixty seven.

His greatest love however was and is Rugby. He watches it—reads about it—and talks about it whenever he has the opportunity to do so. I know as a New Zealander the All blacks are part of his identity and rugby is in his blood.

I feel rugby is more important to him than I am. My watching and trying to understand rugby does not help no matter how many times I try. I feel it is very dangerous. In fact there is now research being carried out in both America and Australia, as to the effect on the brain of its being repeatedly concussed while playing football. This was discussed on 14th May 2012, on Four Corners. ABC. Sydney and it was concluded that permanent harm to the brain including that of children could be caused by repeated concussion through playing football.

Loving Rugby or any of the sports is not part of who I am. Loving music, especially South American music and dancing is not part of who he is either.

The upside of not having such interests in common is we each have more time to pursue our individual interests, which I appreciate.

What I miss is the emotional sharing with him of things such as music which turns me on and at the same time turns him off, dancing, going to the theatre, seminars, short courses and/or conferences. Even though I enjoy going alone I feel how much more enjoyable it would be going with a companion or a partner especially for dancing.

I am disappointed we could not be like the friends of my father who loved dancing and went dancing together every week all through their long married life.

Though I am incapable of sharing his joy and excitement about the All Blacks scoring a try, he is able to share rugby with his cousin and his sister both personally and on the telephone.

I am angry everything seems to revolve around his interests and my interests are ignored.

I believe it is the smell of his body which caused us both to marry in spite of our lack of enough common interests and not being in love with each other.

I feel what is most missing in our relationship is mutual passion except perhaps for politics in which we are both interested and in which we are both on the same side.

I know I am like his mother in looks and attitude and that may have influenced him on a deeper level. He is nothing like my father in looks and attitude and this may be the reason I am not as happy being married to him as he says he is being married to me.

Before we became engaged he used to talk to me about a woman he knew in Wellington.

He read me part of a letter from her in which she told him how much she missed him and their evening brandy together. As she was not of Greek descent, his parents did not approve of this relationship and I suspect this is why he left Wellington to stay with his sister in Sydney after he had qualified as a pharmacist.

He was one of the few educated eligible bachelors of Greek descent in Wellington and was told by one man that he was welcome to marry either of his daughters.

The pressure was on him to marry a Greek girl and love did not enter into the matter at all at that time in the Greek Community when arranged marriages were the norm and marrying for love was very rare especially when the partner was not of Greek origin.

I did not feel Jim and I were friends in spite of the fact he was friendly.

Everything changed between us when he and I were alone in the kitchen at our place and he suddenly kissed me.

I felt like I had had an electric shock.

I felt tingles when he held my hand as he left soon afterwards.

My parents were away and he had asked me to go to the movies with him in the city.

I had asked him to come in for supper after he had driven me home and my sister was out.

We had been seen at the movies by the man who had been my "boyfriend" at school and his then wife, my cousin, because we had not done what my sister and her friends always did.

They went into the theatre when the lights were off and left before they went on again. As we were seen out alone together the news was soon known by all my extended family.

My cousin his brother in law told Jim his mother said there was already a "done deal" between our respective families that I would marry my lawyer friend and warned him to stay away from me. He arranged meetings for him with women he believed were more suitable.

Jim later told me he had to tell one of them he was interested in someone else as he felt her family were about to announce their engagement. As soon as he returned to Wellington he sent me the rejection of me in favour of my sister letter.

Many times he has told me how much he has always regretted sending me that letter.

He told me he had only done so because he had been warned off me.

He told me as he did not know what kind of people were involved he felt even his life could have been threatened.

About eighteen months later after one of the senior lecturers from college had told him he knew a pharmacist in Bondi who needed a locum for six months he came back to Sydney.

He rang me a couple of months later to say he wanted to see me and he would pick me up in his car after he finished work.

As was the custom in the Greek community at that time, relatives or friends of men wanting to get married approached my parents on their behalf to see if we would be interested in them as possible marriage partners. This arrangement is called a "Proxenia" in Greek and I had several of them after I left school and even one in my final year at school.

When he picked me up after work, he drove to Centennial Park. He stopped the car and we got out of the car and sat on a park bench. He said to me "Helen, love has nothing to do with it but I want you to marry me."

I told my mother. She liked the idea however she asked me to wait for a week before I replied because a friend of my father had arranged for a doctor I already knew from our Youth Club to come up from Melbourne to speak to me personally.

I knew I was expected to get married and as my sexual education had consisted mainly of reading Jane Austen novels, I felt I was morally obliged to marry the man who had kissed me so I didn't wait. My mother was very annoyed with me.

When I told my father we were engaged he was very surprised and very pleased.

He did not like any of my other suitors and he very much approved of this one as he knew his family. He had tears of happiness in his eyes as he said to me "We knew we would not have any trouble getting rid of your sister, but we thought we would have trouble getting rid of you."

When I told my mother's sister I was engaged she said "Oh your father has bought you a husband has he?"

When I went up the road to tell my "adopted" aunt (my lawyer friend's real aunt) she told her younger daughter who asked her was I engaged to my lawyer friend—her cousin.

I felt quite startled and embarrassed.

Nevertheless I felt they were happy for me and wished me well unlike the message my real aunt had conveyed to me.

Once we had announced our engagement everything changed for the worse because we did what everyone else suggested we do instead of talking to each other to find out what we really wanted to do.

We were taken by his brother-in-law to a jeweller he knew in order to buy the Diamond Engagement Ring. Nobody asked me did I like diamonds.

I am angry we had to buy a diamond ring because it was what everyone did when they became engaged. Had I been given a choice I would have chosen a large lapis lazulis deep blue gemstone ring.

As I was in my final year of the Kindergarten Teachers course I had a lot to do so I was very glad Jim went back to Wellington after the engagement party which his brother Dino had come by plane from Wellington to attend.

He wrote to me quite often.

His letters were about as romantic and personal as the entries in the white pages of the telephone book and I did not keep any of them.

I decided that during the term holidays I would go to Wellington to break the engagement.

My nose must have interfered with my brain because when I got there I did not want to do so even after while entering the room to meet one of his Irish aunts I heard his mother say: "We preferred the other sister but . . ."

In spite of this I liked his mother, his family, the warmth and the friendliness in their home.

My sense of smell was more persuasive than my pride or my self esteem so I did not break off the engagement. I am angry with myself for not doing so and for accepting his proposal in the first place.

"Love has nothing to do with it but I want you to marry me" was not romantic or emotional. It had come only from his head and not from his heart and I responded from my head and not my heart too. At least neither of us pretended our engagement was anything other than our response to the pressure we felt from the expectation of our parents and the community in which we lived.

In January of the next year he and his family came over to Sydney and we were married in the St Sophia Greek Orthodox Cathedral. Neither of us understood the significance of the wedding ceremony or the meaning of anything the priest had said.

I felt awkward when the priest placed a wreath of wax orange blossom tied together with a white satin ribbon on my head and on Jim's head. The priest started chanting and we and all our attendants had to follow him as he walked around in a circle three times.

After the service and in the office without asking me my occupation he wrote "Domestic duties" as my occupation on the marriage certificate when I had been a student and had just graduated as a Kindergarten Teacher.

I regret not telling him he had made a mistake and could he please correct it there and then.

The Wedding Reception was a celebration party for my parents, relatives and their friends.

His parents knew nobody there except for their son and their daughters so very soon after we went to Wellington they held another Wedding Reception for their relatives and friends there.

At least at the Sydney party there was one table at which some of my friends and cousins were seated and from the official table I could see them and all the weddings guests most of whom I had known since I was a child.

At the party in Wellington I did not know anyone including the man to whom I was married. From the official table I looked at a room full of completely unfamiliar people most of whom I had never even seen before.

After we had become engaged I asked him where he thought we could go on our honeymoon and he said "I leave it all to you." which was not at all helpful.

I was disappointed he showed no interest in any of the arrangements and had left them all to me.

I feel angry with myself for not challenging him at the time by insisting on finding out what his preferences were.

I had booked a double room in a hotel close to where the reception was being held.

The room was an inside room with no windows. It was not the attractive modern room with a double bed I had expected. It was a dark, musty old fashioned room with twin beds.

His best man had been giving him brandy to help him get through the day.

After he had called out to me several times while I was in the bathroom he went to sleep.

During my teens I had read romantic love stories and my wedding night memories keep reminding me "love has nothing to do" with our relationship—certainly not romantic love.

I am angry for the unfulfilment of my dreams and his complete lack of empathy, sensitivity and understanding.

While he slept I stayed up all night writing letters to friends and relatives thanking them for their attendance and for their wedding gifts.

I do not remember whether or not we had breakfast in the morning.

All I remember is feeling embarrassed because there was an announcement of our wedding and a photo of us in one of the daily newspapers. I was afraid people who read the paper might recognise us so I wore my dark sunglasses.

Later that morning our families met us at to the airport to see us off on our honeymoon.

I was sleep deprived and wearing a black dress which reflected my mood.

His father had tears in his eyes when he kissed me on the cheek and he looked very unwell.

I felt sad and unhappy and it did not feel at all to me like a happy occasion worth celebrating.

I was not looking forward to going away with a man I felt was a stranger.

At our destination I wanted to go and explore the island.

He was not interested in coming with me and said "I don't like Islands."

As we had not discussed where we would like to spend our honeymoon and he had left it all to me I had chosen an island which sounded exotic and exciting.

I was disappointed and frustrated by his negative response.

I am angry he left everything to me and then did not like what I had chosen.

This ruined for me what could have been a happy and interesting holiday.

I felt unhappy because of his attitude and I felt self-conscious and ugly wearing the dresses made by my mother's dressmaker.

What sort of dress sense could I have had even had my mother allowed me to chose my own clothes when in my formative years my role models were nuns in habits and ready made clothes did not fit me?

I felt angry and betrayed by the nuns from whom I had received the impression that how one dressed and how one looked was not important.

In the real world after school in which I now was, how one dressed and how one looked was the most important criterion on which one was judged by others and how one felt about oneself.

We had our own private hut and every night we joined other people in the dining room.

Dance music was playing and I wanted to dance however I just sat there tapping my right foot in time to the music while he chatted with the man next to him at the group table.

I did not ask him to dance as it was not acceptable for a woman to ask a man to dance with her at that time. I am angry at the complete lack of a feeling of togetherness I had for the whole time we were there. I felt there was nothing I could do about it and just had to put up with how it was.

He seemed to spend a lot of time watching the blonde lady in her Bikini sitting on the beach. I knew he loved swimming so I assumed he would have gone swimming had he been with anyone other than me. I was not only too embarrassed to be seen in a swim suit I could not swim and hated the feel of cold water on my skin. I felt he must have been as frustrated and as unhappy about my not liking to swim as I was about the fact he did not like to dance.

From going to the movies and reading novels I had an unrealistic view of love and marriage.

I had never been out with boys. I had two or three friends who were boys but had never had a boyfriend so nothing had prepared me for being in the situation I was in.

The honeymoon was such a disaster we both agreed to cut it short and go back to Sydney earlier than planned.

After a few days in Sydney my extended family and some friends came to the wharf to wave us good bye and throw streamers to us as we stood at the rail of the ship on our way to our new life in Wellington.

The trip back to New Zealand I have almost completely erased from my memory.

The only thing I clearly remember is having to fill in a questionnaire before we left the ship.

One question was "In what country were your parents born?"

As I had put "Greece" I was separated from Jim and had to join the "Aliens" line.

For the whole three years we were living in New Zealand I felt like an alien and went back home to Sydney whenever and as often as I could.

We had no choice about what kind of house we lived in or in which part of Wellington we lived as his father had already put a deposit on a house for us as a wedding present.

Even though we both disliked living in it we lived there for almost a year.

His younger sister worked for him at the pharmacy which was open Monday to Thursdays 9am till 6pm and Fridays 9am to 9pm.

He used to pick Celia up on his way to work and take her home afterwards when we were living in Wellington until we rented a house in Belmont which was closer to the pharmacy.

I was on my own and had a lot of time to myself however I did not feel free.

I felt I was in prison. I felt like an outsider, unwanted, unloved, unappreciated, isolated and invalidated because I felt I was not free to be myself.

I was very unhappy I could not tell anyone how I was feeling and nobody cared.

One of my cousins had married and moved to another state. I looked forward to receiving her letters as they cheered me up because I liked her sense of humour.

I sensed Jim was unhappy too. He would not let me talk to him and he did not talk to me about his feelings.

He had to live in a house he hated with an alien woman who did not want to be there and he was running his own business in an unfamiliar suburb he did not like.

At least he was in his own country and he was surrounded by his family and his relatives.

I had no relatives, friends or acquaintances in Wellington.

I missed my family, relatives, friends and even the familiar faces of complete strangers.

I missed the feeling of space, the buildings, the landmarks, the sunshine and the lack of extreme cold, wind and rain.

I missed the sound of familiar voices and the familiar accents.

Most of all I missed my lawyer friend and I dreamed of him every single night I was living in Wellington. I wondered whether this was because I missed him or whether my dreaming of him was a symbol for everything else I was missing in my life which now felt so empty.

I was very glad to see him when we accidentally met on my first visit back to Sydney when Celia had come too.

He had married the girl about whom he used to talk most to me and he invited me to lunch at their flat and gave me a lift to the city in the taxi he took back to work.

He was a year older than I and we met in our early teens when our families were holidaying in Katoomba. When he moved to Sydney for his tertiary education he lived for over a year with his uncle and his family just up the road from where we lived.

We spent hours talking on the phone or having coffee or going to committee meetings or working on the monthly magazine of our Youth Club.

After I had listened to him and one of the other boys talking about their problems with girls I realised how badly growing up with culture conflict was affecting some of the boys as well as most of the girls.

The extroverts just disregarded the rules and did their own thing anyway.

The introverts had a harder time as they obeyed the rules and lived their lives accordingly.

The rule for the girls was they did not go out alone with any boy especially an Australian one while they were single.

The rules for the boys were they were allowed to go out with Australian girls but not marry them. They were to marry only Greek girls however they were not allowed to go out with them until the marriage had been arranged.

This situation ended in some mixed outcomes.

In one case I remember one man had been going out with an Australian girl for some time.

His arranged marriage to a Greek girl ended in divorce within the year and he then married the Australian woman he loved despite opposition from his parents.

In another case a Greek Australian girl was engaged to a Greek man and when she found out that his Australian girlfriend was pregnant to him she broke off the engagement.

Another woman of Greek descent climbed out of the bathroom window on what was to be her wedding day to the man chosen by her parents and ran away with the man she loved who was waiting for her nearby.

The existence of our youth club gave us much more freedom socially

There were cases where the parents broke up liaisons of which they did not approve which were formed in the club while others of which they did approve led to marriage.

In the first year of our club the parents used to come to all the dances, sit on chairs near the dance floor and look at who was dancing with whom.

We thought perhaps it was to make sure their son or daughter did not dance too many times with the same partner. Thankfully this did not last very long before they abandoned this supervision and we had a lot more freedom.

In spite of the freedom I was too self conscious to socialise with anyone other than on a one to one basis in which I was the one who did the listening until I met my uncle Basil who was not a relative but a friend of one of my older male cousins.

During my teenage years my lawyer friend came to all the monthly dances. He and two or three boys asked me to dance because even though I was overweight I was "light as a feather" when I was dancing I was told.

At that time my lawyer friend was part of every significant happening in my life.

He was there at our club revues when I either played the piano or sang or did both.

He was part of the group with whom we were allowed to go to the theatre, or the movies at night whenever his aunt bought the tickets.

He was part of the holidays in Katoomba where we used to spend the Easter and Christmas holidays playing Five hundred or Monopoly at his aunt's family home.

A couple of times we spent New Year's Eve at Echo Point where one year stands out in my memory as we were allowed to go to the dance held in the Restaurant down there.

Some people may have considered we were an "Item".

To me he was a friend and the only brother I ever had. I was as close to him as Jim is with his younger sister Celia and Connie who is only thirteen months older and lives in Sydney.

As my lawyer friend's family of origin came from the same Greek Island from which my mother's father had originated it is quite possible we were in fact related in one of the past generations.

I did like him and I felt he liked me. I had the feeling of togetherness with him even after we both married. As then two childless couples Jim and I and he and his wife went out to a night club with two other couples who left straight after dinner. The four of us stayed on to dance all night then had breakfast at Kings Cross in the morning which was fun and a very memorable and exciting occasion at least for me if not for Jim.

I liked the sound of his voice and the shape of his face and his positive attitude which probably reminded me of my father. What I did not like which I discovered the first time he sat next to me in the car was the smell of his body. I liked the fact he was a lawyer. We were both on the committee of our youth club as were two other boys doing law.

In the photo taken of the committee I was surprised to find later that I was sitting with the three lawyers when at the time I was doing kindergarten teacher training.

Even though I felt emotionally close to him I did not like his smell so he could never have been a possible father for my future children which fact I did not know at the time.

What I had expected when I married was going out every night and having fun with my husband.

I did not anticipate that Jim would dislike going out with me and would prefer to stay home or be with his family of origin. Neither did it occur to me there would not be much opportunity for having fun in Wellington.

I knew being on his feet all day he would be tired and needed time to rest however I felt it was because he didn't like me or enjoy being with me that he did not ask me what I would like to do on any occasion I can remember.

I just fitted in as best I could with him and just did what he wanted to do.

The coffee shop which served light meals and which we both liked was in the city and closed at 6pm. The pharmacy also closed at 6pm.

Going out for dinner consisted of my taking the train to the city in time to get to the coffee shop before it closed and order the Veal Sausages for the three of us. I would wait until Jim had closed the pharmacy and had driven with Celia into town to meet me.

I found this quite stressful as there was always the worry of whether they would get there in time. After dinner on a couple of occasions the three of us went to a Symphony Concert at the Town Hall.

I felt angry, frustrated and unhappy most of the time I lived in Wellington.

I had not found there any Adult Education classes like the ones in psychology, dispute resolution, assertiveness training, mosaic tiling, oil painting, acrylic painting, Chinese painting and Italian and Spanish language classes I later found in Sydney.

In spite of having absolutely no aptitude for languages I enjoyed going to Italian and Spanish classes as I liked how they sounded. I am angry with myself for not persevering long enough to learn to speak a few words in either of them. Jim refused to go to any classes so I did not have enough motivation to keep going by myself.

Had we not moved to Sydney I know I could never had done what I feel I was born to do and most enjoyed doing and that was having babies and passing university exams.

Everything from the time of our engagement convinced me not only was there no love in our relationship but we both had married primarily in order to please our parents.

I feel my strong feelings of wanting him to be the father of my children had an effect on him too and is the reason why he asked me to marry him in the first place.

He had and still has a very strong emotional bond with his family of origin and was and still is very protective of his two sisters the only members of it who are still alive.

I too had always felt protective of my parents especially of my mother.

I remember often having to miss school and later Kindergarten Training College in order to look after her when she was sick. One lasting effect of my looking after my mother when she was having a bilious attack is my intense dislike of the colour yellow.

I remember when I was thirteen sitting in the hospital waiting room while my mother had her gall bladder removed. I also remember how much I appreciated the surgeon's coming out of the operating theatre to tell me the operation was over and my mother was in recovery and was OK. I am angry I had to go through that experience alone and wonder where my father was at that time?

Jim's mother told us more than once that we deserved each other.

As an extrovert herself she did not understand introverts in general or her elder son in particular as he was the only one in the family who was more introverted than extroverted.

I wondered if she was right and we were destined to marry. Had his sister not married my cousin I probably would never have even met him.

Had my parents not approved of him I know I would not have gone ahead.

He told me if his parents had not approved of me he would not have gone ahead either.

It seems we had pleased our parents and their approval was more important to him and to me than our being happy together.

As a qualified pharmacist Jim could have worked in London as some of his friends were and as he would have liked to be doing too. As his father was very ill and dying of cancer leaving him at that time was out of the question.

What made matters more stressful for him was the fact my father had advised him to buy a business of his own as soon as possible and he had taken my father's advice.

The only pharmacy for sale at the time was in Lower Hutt a suburb away from the city of Wellington where he had always lived. He did not like working in an unfamiliar suburb.

When we sold our house and rented one in a quiet leafy area up a hill and closer to his work it was even worse for him as we were further away from the city and his family and even more isolated than we were before.

I often wondered if it was all my fault I was unhappy or was it because he had told me from the beginning "Love has nothing to do with it" when he asked me to marry him?

There was no intellectual stimulation, no excitement, nowhere to go especially at night in Wellington and there was no friendship, passion, emotional connection or intimacy in our relationship. His favourite song was and still is "You Were Meant For Me" and his playing that song especially for me is the most romantic thing I can remember he has ever done and this only happened recently.

When I suggested in the first year of our marriage that we go to counselling he said "I am happily married so if you are not it is your problem not mine."

The only time I felt happy was when I went back to Sydney and was away from Wellington and away from him.

I will always be grateful and indebted to my father for having transferred a small investment property of his into my name before I was married. The rent from this property enabled me to make trips home and to pay for my education and psychotherapy without having to ask my husband for the money. Without my own money I feel I could not have survived being married and living away from Sydney for the three years we lived in Wellington.

As my parents did not seem happy to have me back home I did not stay for very long.

I kept going back to Wellington thinking the marriage would improve when we had a baby.

As we were not becoming pregnant I wanted and needed to know the reason why.

The first gynaecologist I consulted told me there was no physical reason he could find why I was unable to become pregnant. He told me he suspected there may be a psychological reason and referred me to a psychiatrist who practised as a psychotherapist/psychoanalyst.

I spent a few weeks freely associating while I was lying on the couch and he sat behind my head. After we had discussed my dreams he told me I needed to go to University.

I had repressed this long held desire so I had done nothing to make it possible. Now he had told me this I knew I needed to go back to Sydney to study in order to matriculate before I could go to University and this is what I decided to do.

We also consulted the leading Gynaecologist/Obstetrician in Wellington who told us we would never have children because he could see from the pattern of hair on my legs that I was hypo-pituitary. As I could smell liquor on his breath I did not believe anything he told us. Somehow other people knew what he had said and when I went to Sydney one of my cousins said to me "I am so sorry because I know how much you love children."

I am angry the doctors we consulted in Wellington did not test Jim before they reached any conclusion as to why we were not able to conceive. It was only when we had moved to Sydney and consulted my mother's doctor who tested Jim's blood that we found Jim was lacking in Vitamin D which was easily remedied and the physical problem in the marriage was solved.

The emotional problem in the marriage did not go away as I had not forgotten the letter.

When we first came back to live in Sydney we stayed at my family home for a few months while my parents were in Japan to which they had travelled on a cargo ship which also took a few passengers.

On the results of an IQ test I was given a Provisional Matric and I was at University feeling like a fish out of water for the whole three month term I was there. I had enrolled in the Faculty of Medicine and as I had not done any chemistry, physics or zoology at school I could listen to the lectures and take notes however I could not do any of the practical classes.

When in the physics prac. the lecturer said "take out your micrometer screw gauge"—I not only did not have one I had no idea what it was. When in zoology prac. we were told to dissect the vagus nerve I found out by asking the boy next to me I had cut it out.

Jim had failed in only one subject when he did Medicine at the University of Otago in NZ. and was not given a post or allowed to carry that subject and had to repeat the whole year. I had only enrolled in medicine because he was repeating first year medicine in Sydney and I thought it would give us more in common and bring us closer together if I did medicine too.

Instead of this being the case he accused me of being there to spy on him and quit straight away while I forced myself to stay until the end of the term.

I achieved nothing academically or spiritually by being there however I had done what he had asked me to do in his rejection letter and that was to help him to get to know my sister.

While I was at Uni he had ample opportunity to ask my sister who was still single to go out with him. To my knowledge he did not do so except the one time about which he told me.

He told me at the time it had been very hot day and my sister had said to him "I am going for a swim. Do you want to come?" and they went to the baths in Coogee.

Had he really wanted to marry her this was his chance to make it happen. As he had convinced me that is what he wanted to do by sending me the rejection letter I did not understand why he was not taking this opportunity to do something about it.

I wondered if the reason he told me he wrote the rejection letter was the truth or whether it was his Catholic education which was stopping him from doing what he really wanted to do.

When recently I asked my sister whether she knew about his parent's letter in which they had asked for her as a marriage partner for him she just exclaimed "But he liked you!"

Why I am angry is because Jim would not let me talk to him about why I was unhappy when we were first married and he has refused to discuss it or let me talk about my feelings since. I feel had we been able to talk about my feelings when we were first married and had seen a therapist then I might have been as happily married to him as he said he was to me.

Despite lack of what I feel is real communication between us I am glad we stayed together.

I feel I could not have become me without him.

I feel he would not have become who he is either had he not married me.

I am not sure that was the best outcome either of us could have achieved with someone else.

I feel we helped each other to develop and grow. I feel we have a good parallel marriage in spite of having some innate and irreconcilable incompatibilities.

He had refused to see a counsellor without at least talking about it while we were living in Wellington. He seemed to be so completely lacking in empathy and did not seem to understand or care about how I was feeling and why I felt we needed to seek professional help. He dismissed psychology as rubbish and refused to read any books which I felt may have helped us.

I am angry he was and still is nearly always negative in attitude about nearly everything.

His mother told me he was such a difficult baby she had felt like throwing him out of the window at times so perhaps his negativity is an inborn characteristic he can't control.

I am angry he distanced himself from any possible problem in our relationship and blamed me for my own unhappiness thus avoiding taking any of the responsibility himself.

I know my own attitude certainly had a lot to do with the problems in the marriage.

I trace the feeling of my being rejected in favour of my sister to the time when she was born.

I under-estimated the fact that everything else in my life had also changed at that time and that happy outgoing babies are more attractive to most people than the introverted ones.

I did not realise this did not mean I had been entirely displaced by my sister and moreover it did not mean everyone would always prefer her to me as I then mistakenly believed.

It was only when I learned about Cognitive Behaviour Therapy that I realised how I had been thinking caused how I felt. It was only when I learned to challenge the truth of what I was thinking that I changed how I was feeling and stopped creating self-fulfilling prophesies.

The only time I felt less unhappy when I lived in Wellington is when I was working at a private kindergarten for six months. Jim and his parents disapproved of my looking after other people's children and when his father died I felt under pressure to stop working so I stopped.

I tried working with Jim at the pharmacy which was not a good idea as I did not like serving customers and unpacking orders. I felt like a complete misfit in that environment.

Staying home and doing household jobs and cooking did not work either.

He did not like my cooking and still doesn't and he preferred and still prefers his own.

He did not like the way I washed and ironed his shirts and preferred to do these things for himself which is fortunate for me as I am not interested in or good at doing these things.

As I could not take on the housewife role I was forced to find another.

After I had seen the psychoanalyst and found out I still needed to go to University then I knew I had to sit the Leaving Certificate again and I was very happy to have a reason to leave Jim and his country to go back home to Sydney to study.

At that time I felt it would be better for both of us to separate and later divorce.

As soon as I was in Sydney I sent him the diamond engagement ring by post and felt that was the end of the marriage. I did not feel I was really married at all and could not bring myself to even think of him or refer to him as my husband.

When he received the ring he must have been feeling desperate.

He told me it was Saturday and his day off so he rang the psychoanalyst who told him to come to his home that afternoon.

After listening to him he told me the psychoanalyst said to him "Your wife will never come back to you on her own. If you want to stay married to her you need to go to Sydney to persuade her to come back with you."

To my surprise that is what he did. I met him on his arrival in Sydney.

He had not only come to Sydney he seemed to have changed in his attitude towards me.

We were so engrossed in talking to each other we did not even notice the taxi was taking us to the right street in the wrong suburb.

He had told my parents if it turned out I did not like living in Wellington he would sell the pharmacy and come to live in Sydney permanently when we were first engaged.

Maybe by sending him back the engagement ring and staying away for so long I had told him if not in words that I would never be happy living in Wellington.

I was used to coming to Sydney for a short time then go back to Wellington on my own and this time it was very different.

I don't know whose idea it was that my sister come back with us and we fly to Auckland then take the bus to Rotorua but that is what we did. We stayed in Rotorua for two days. After we did some sight seeing I watched while Jim and my sister went for a swim in the Blue Baths,.

I felt they were the couple and I was the odd person out.

The only thing I enjoyed in Rotorua was the Maori Concert at the Hotel that night.

Next day we flew to Wellington in a small plane which only accommodated five passengers.

I was glad Lil had brought her guitar with her as I had discovered a small recording studio not far from where we lived. I persuaded her to bring her guitar and come with me to record both a Maori song Haere Mai and some Greek folk songs.

We sang the songs together while she strummed on her guitar which was a Spanish one. The man who made the recording offered us a job. He said our voices blended so well he would like us to be part of a concert group which entertained the troops overseas if we were interested.

I had gone through a stage when I had made recordings accompanied by a pianist and then by the Greek band which used to play at our youth club dances.

After I had sung in the University Review accompanied by a Jazz Trio the leader of the group asked me would I like to make a recording with them when they were rehearsing next day at the recording studio. We recorded "St Louis Blues" and "You came along" and I loved singing with the jazz trio as the recording sounded much more professional than any of my other acetate recordings. I had done nothing with my singing after that.

When a friend whom I had not seen for some time said to me "What are you doing with your singing?" I took all my acetate recordings to

EMI in the city and paid to have them made into a CD. I gave him one of the copies to which my sister told me everyone had to listen at the dinner at his home to which my sister had been invited.

The technician at EMI who had made the CD said to me "Do you know you could have been a professional singer?"

At no stage of my life did I want to be a professional singer even though I loved to sing.

I am angry I did not feel like singing after I was married and singing was no longer part of my life. Swimming which he loved stopped being part of his life when he married me.

This is the price we each had to pay for not marrying someone with whom we shared these interests.

My sister's visit temporarily rekindled my desire to sing and we were both pleased we had been offered a job even though it did not interest either of us.

Years later when I was doing the counselling and psychotherapy course I asked my sister to write about some of her experiences so I could include what she wrote in my major work.

She agreed to help me as had some of my friends and cousins and I included their stories in my assignment which I felt made it more interesting.

The following quotation is part of what my sister had written:

"When I went back to Wellington with Helen after she had come back to Sydney for a while, it was July and I nearly froze to death. I refused to get up in the morning until Helen had run me a hot bath so I could warm up before getting dressed. Helen was miserable so I felt miserable too.

Her neighbour invited us in for morning tea but Helen made me go on my own.

Helen would not go because the neighbour had lots of cats and the house smelled.

A woman rang the doorbell one day and she was Australian and she had heard Helen was Australian too.

For at least the next half hour she talked non-stop about how she hated New Zealand and did not want to die there. She wanted to lie flat in her grave and it was too hilly in Wellington.

When Helen and I went to some ballroom dancing lessons I met a lady from England who wanted me to have morning tea with her as she had no friends and wanted to go back home.

It didn't sound like a very happy place to me. It was always windy and cold. No one could stand around street corners chatting or they would either be blown away or be frozen to the spot. I could see Helen wasn't happy. She was stuck in the house as she couldn't drive.

She spent her time cooking meals. Sometimes his sister would come for lunch too. They would chat about the pharmacy and clients and Helen would be excluded from the conversation—then they would leave and we would clean up and get dinner ready.

I knew this wouldn't last. Helen was sure to go on strike.

To make matters worse, Helen and Jim had consulted the leading Gynaecologist in Wellington. He told them that Helen was hypo-pituitary and could never have children.

I wish Helen could have taken her children back to Wellington a few years later and personally confronted this man.

When Jim realised Helen would never be happy in Wellington he sold the pharmacy and settled in Sydney after they had been overseas for four months.

Growing up in two cultures was not easy. At home we had to be Greek with all its restrictions. In the Greek community everyone knew everyone else so we had to be careful that we did not 'disgrace' the family.

At school, I wanted to fit into the Australian community. I heard the girls talking about boys and parties and generally having a normal teenage life.

We could only go out as a family to social functions. The excitement of the week was going to the movies or going to church.

I rebelled and did what I wanted to do thus breaking all the rules.

Helen used to express her rebellion by yelling and slamming doors and always complied with the rules. I felt it was natural for me to seek male company. As we had no brothers and we were not encouraged to mix with boys and girls who were not Greek, I used to go out with boys secretly."

As an introvert and the first born I believed rules were important and needed to be observed so I felt what she was doing was wrong. I felt God would punish her in some way at some time in her life for breaking the rules and God would reward me in some way at some time in my life for not having broken them.

Whether this was part of the Catholic indoctrination I had received at school or whether it is innate and part of who I am I do not know. No matter what the cause I am probably unable to ever break free from that kind of thinking and feeling.

In spite of all my anger I am very grateful for all the blessings in my life no matter how or why they have come about.

They are far greater in significance and importance and outweigh all my losses and all my actual or perceived deprivations.

When we moved to Sydney permanently I felt much happier than I had ever felt when we were living in Wellington.

I am not sure Jim felt he had made the right decision or that he liked living in Sydney instead of living in his own country. He often tells me how much he misses the hills in Wellington, the twilight and the lack of humidity, traffic and pollution.

When he told me recently "If anyone were to ask me whether looking back I would change anything in my life I would say *'Yes. I would change 90% to 95% of everything in my life. The only thing I would not change is marrying Helen. That is the best decision I ever made and I will cherish it till the end.'*"

I assume from his saying this to me he was not sorry he had made the move to Sydney.

I feel marrying him was the right thing to do in spite of sometimes asking myself how did I get into this situation?

At the time I felt I did the right thing to listen to and be guided by my intuition.

At times I have been attracted to various other men however I could never imagine my being married to anyone other than Jim.

I do not understand why a marriage which is not based on romantic love seems to be regarded as inferior in Australia which has adopted the Hollywood style marriage as the norm.

I feel abnormal because I have never experienced being "in love" and I do not understand what people who are in love actually feel or how they behave.

From reading the novel Anna Karenina by Tolstoy I gained the impression being in love was a very dangerous state in which to be. It can lead to tragic consequences and ruin lives.

I can not imagine people marrying not knowing anything more about that person other than the fact they are sexually attracted to him or her.

I can't imagine marrying against the wishes of the other person's family or my own family, which is another example of culture conflict or perhaps personal immaturity on my part.

I am in favour of arranged marriages if the parties themselves are interested even though passion and excitement may be missing.

Arranged marriages were the norm for centuries and are still accepted in many parts of the world. What are rightly now unacceptable and criminal in Australia, are forced marriages.

Jim frequently points out to me we are still married while many people who married for love have long since been divorced. Divorce is more acceptable and is more common than it used to be. I wonder however whether enough research has been done on what the real effect of divorce is on the children involved.

Initially I felt divorce was the best course for both Jim and me. I am glad after moving to Sydney to live, my mind and my feelings changed.

Having our children and jointly bringing them up is what we most have in common and binds us together forever no matter what the future may hold for either of us.

5

PSYCHOTHERAPY

Psychotherapy is supposed to help people overcome their emotional problems by being listened to by a person who has been trained to listen reflectively with unconditional love and support.

At the Jansen Newman Institute we were told our role with clients was to listen without judgment and not to make a diagnosis or give any advice.

I have personally found that the only times I have been helped by going to a psychotherapist has been when a diagnosis has been made and I have been able to work out how to proceed.

I wonder why the psychotherapist's role is not like that of a doctor who listens to your symptoms, make a diagnosis and gives you a prescription which will fix the problem.

Why is an emotional problem usually treated so differently from a physical problem?

The psychiatrist I was sent to see by the gynaecologist I had consulted when we were first married and lived in Wellington worked as a psychotherapist/analyst.

Without his telling me my problem was an unfulfilled need and desire to go to university I am sure I would not have embarked on the course of study which resulted in four university degrees, four diplomas and numerous certificates of attendance at further education classes.

After reading Betty Friedan's book The Feminine Mystique in 1963 I realised I was not the only married woman with children living in a comfortable home who was not happy or feeling fulfilled by her homemaker role and lifestyle.

My sister was happy with looking after her husband, her home and her children, playing golf and tennis, being a member of a book club and being the president of the women's committee at her sons' school.

Other women married with children were happy with having regular appointments with their hairdresser, their beautician, manicurist and podiatrist and keeping up with the latest fashion by reading the Women's magazines.

All these women also appeared to have an active social life and seemed to be happy.

Women who worked outside the home were rare and met with the disapproval of most of them it seemed to me.

I am angry with myself for not fitting the happy and well adjusted married woman profile.

I was not interested in any of the things which interested the women I knew and I felt I was the odd person out. I felt there was something very wrong with me and I sought help from therapists.

I am angry that after spending so much time and so much of my father's money on seeing psychotherapists over the years only some of them were helpful in other ways and none of them really helped me with my weight problem which is still with me.

The most helpful in this regard was the woman I call the good psychologist.

At my request she gave me a written account of her perception of my weight problem and what may be contributing to it and what may hinder or help me resolve it.

Her report is three pages long and I still read it to check what if any progress I have made.

I presented as an intelligent, self-aware person who had been struggling with the effects of yo-yo dieting, binge eating and a tendency to adopt or try out any weight loss program which offered me a resolution to this long term problem. I seemed interested and committed to the process of exploring the meaning of this struggle and how my use of food and my self image rendered me 'stuck' on the merry-go-round of dieting and putting on weight.

She said my weight was a result of my genetic, social and psychological history and the way in which I coped with my social and family environment.

In her opinion I had used my fat on an unconscious level at various times in my life in order to be able to survive threats to my basic self from the attitudes and behaviour of other people.

It seemed to her I had had a family background of both physical and emotional abuse coming mainly from my mother who was unhappy in herself and unable to mother me in the way I needed to be mothered. Indoctrinated in the Catholic faith I believed I was responsible for my suffering while my identity refused to accept this. She believes I resolved this essential split by developing my mind at the expense of my body.

Eating was a way of both comforting myself and giving myself the pleasure I needed.

In addition it served to give me a sense of autonomy by allowing me to be rebellious in an acceptable way.

As I got older I protected myself against my developing sexuality, any expression of which was prohibited in the community in which I lived by believing my body was unacceptable.

My being fat resolved the conflict between the real me and the socially constructed me.

Another area of inner conflict had been the feeling I should have been born a boy and being treated as his son by my father. My going to work resolved this conflict as going to work meant being more like my father and being less like my mother. However in the world of work I was more exposed to my own and to other peoples feelings and desires.

To accept and acknowledge my feelings could have threatened my sense of self and integrity as well as cause problems in the marriage.

Leaving the workforce was one way of avoiding dealing with these issues while provoking others. Both consciously and unconsciously there was a split between my needs and the ability of my family relationship or work to meet them.

I believed my husband's needs were more important than my own and a balance between the two was not possible.

This was reinforced by the fact that when I was fulfilling myself by working outside the home my husband became ill and I had to give up work in order to look after him.

At the same time I described problems in the relationship such as difficulties communicating and having no interests in common which made it difficult for me to find it fulfilling to stay home and to put the relationship first.

This tended to place me in the victim role which I found it easy to rationalise and difficult from which to escape.

In order to transcend this sort of situation I needed to:

Change my belief system;

Challenge some of the accompanying presuppositions;

Commit myself to using non-food strategies as my primary way of dealing with stress;

Resolve problems of boredom or lack of fulfilment;

Accept my inner self; and

Develop a psychological part of myself which would be my own best friend.

She ended the report by saying we needed to talk further about all the above matters and she looked forward to working with me on the issues with which I felt she could help.

I agreed with her intellectually however emotionally I did not at first accept that either of my parents, especially my mother had been abusive with me in any way.

Like many survivors of abusive situations I saw her behaviour as normal.

I am not angry with my mother as I empathised with her.

I knew when she hit me or called me names it was because she was stressed and unhappy and she was taking it out on me.

I felt she was not angry with me personally but she needed to release some of the tension which was the result of her life situation not only something I had done which had upset her.

By taking these feelings out of the equation and looking at the matter objectively I can see my mother was in fact physically and emotionally abusive to me.

As I copied her way of coping by yelling I too am guilty of being abusive to our children particularly the younger three. I am sorry I did not realise at the time that coping by yelling was abusive to the children.

Having the psychologist's report to which I could refer whenever I wished made her actual presence and working with her in person unnecessary for me so I stopped seeing her.

I believe another factor in my decision to discontinue working with her was that at this time I was notified her fees were going up and as I had not expected such a thing to happen I was not able to adjust to this new situation and left therapy instead.

When I went to my then GP the next time I felt I was in need of help he said "When the load is breaking your back you need to lighten the load or find someone to help you carry it." He suggested I see the psychologist who had been recommended to him by one of his colleagues.

The "the last card in the pack" as she referred to herself in her report back to the doctor, was a psychologist who was a chain smoker.

I saw her for about three months as I felt I needed her support to complete a Project Report "Marriage in Some Hollywood films: Changing Aspects of Sexism."

I had been doing Film Studies for four years as the Music course was no longer available. As I had completed Women's Studies in the meantime I could approach it in a different way and I finally graduated as Master of General Studies which degree I found later was not Internationally recognised and was eventually discontinued.

Even though she had smoked through every session with the windows closed I felt the risk to me from her smoking was not great because I was only there for one hour a week for about twelve weeks. It did not occur to me at the time I could have asked her not to smoke during our sessions.

I am angry with myself putting up with something I did not like instead of telling her how I felt. In hindsight I can see that was not helpful to either her or to me though at the time I felt I was doing the right thing.

As I still had not solved my eating problem I asked for another referral several years later.

This time, it was to a male psychologist.

For the first appointment I arrived on time and was surprised to find the front door half open so I went into the small waiting room. I stood and waited for about ten minutes before he arrived. He did not apologise or give me any explanation as to why he was late. He opened the door to his room and asked me to sit down and we started the session.

As the same thing happened again and again with my waiting for about half an hour on the third occasion with no explanation, I stopped making appointments to see him.

On reflection, I feel I had assumed the aim of his behaviour was to get rid of me as a client and I am angry with myself for not confronting him or at least trying to find out more about his motivation before I just quit.

Several years earlier when I had asked my obstetrician for a referral about my over—eating he referred me to a psychiatrist he had known from medical school.

This psychiatrist's style was to write down everything I said. No eye contact. No personal interaction and he did not say much at all.

When on one occasion I asked him to read to me what he had written, my instant reaction was to say to myself "I didn't say that." He had put what I had said in a shortened form and in his own words. I barely recognised his words had the same meaning as what I had said.

As I felt no rapport with him I stopped going to see him as soon as I felt I could do without the regular appointments which gave my life the structure I needed at that time.

We had had our youngest child and this doctor did not seem to have any objection to my taking the baby with me to my appointments.

It was not till our last session that I realised he had a slight speech impediment and then I understood why he had been writing rather than talking during our sessions.

I felt seeing him regularly for about twelve months was beneficial as I did enjoy the train rides and I did need to talk with an adult even though the conversation was one sided.

I was feeling very stressed at that time as having the last two children proved to be a lot more difficult than I had anticipated.

I felt worn out as "Miff" who was there for the first five had died and I could not find anyone to replace her.

I am angry there was no child care or emotional and physical support available to me and I felt I was being punished for having had more children.

Between the fifth and sixth child I had had a miscarriage. Nobody had told me if there was any bleeding I had to go straight to hospital. The bleeding started at midnight after I had had a hectic day. I kept thinking if I was having a miscarriage and waited long enough the foetus would be expelled and the bleeding would stop.

I found out later I had been in shock and semi-conscious when I arrived by ambulance at the hospital just after six o'clock that morning. I had to have several blood transfusions and my doctor told me had I waited two minutes longer it would have been too late.

I had only suspected I was pregnant as it had not been confirmed.

I was feeling some hormonal imbalance and had been sleeping on the couch in the living room.

Since midnight when the bleeding had started, I had been using nappies to soak up the blood and had been putting them in the washing machine. I was taking another nappy to the laundry when I collapsed in the hall. Luckily for me Jim had woken to go to the bathroom and found me. He rang the doctor who told him to call an ambulance and he would see me in the hospital.

My blood pressure was down to "bedrock" and the doctors could not find a pulse they said.

I said to one of the sisters "I feel like fainting" and she said "there is no point in fainting as you are already lying down."

When I lost consciousness, I could still hear what the sisters were saying as I looked down from above at myself and them dressed in blue, around me.

I heard one of the doctors say "I think we are winning now" as I came back.

I had had to stay in hospital for three days and wave to the children from the window as they were not allowed to come into the hospital to visit me.

I am angry with myself for being so stupid and causing so much trouble. I am angry with Jim because I had nearly died and he had slept through almost the entire incident.

As I was still unhappy with my body, I later consulted a nutritionist who referred me to a woman psychiatrist who not only listened to me but interacted with me unlike the previous one I had consulted. She also offered me drugs which I refused.

When I told her I was unhappily married and told her some of the history and how I felt my husband preferred my sister to me, she said "but he married you didn't he?"

I felt she did not understand as she had probably never heard of the song "One has my name and the other has my heart" or know how the wife in that situation must have felt.

She further showed she did not understand me by saying "if you want to have an affair, go and have an affair."

She asked to see my husband and he did see her on one occasion.

What she said to him while I was in the room was "She needs to go to work outside the house and you have to make sure she does by physically dragging her there if necessary."

She did not suggest how I could possibly go to work when we had seven children and I had no help with home or childcare except from my husband before and after work on weekdays, half of Saturdays and all day Sunday.

I knew I needed more intellectual stimulation and the company of adults and the best I could do at that time was to keep studying by going to evening lectures from 6pm to 9pm twice a week with the help of a series of baby sitters till my husband got home about 6.30pm.

I felt then and I feel now that the only way women can really "have it all" is when Genesis 1 ultimately replaces Genesis 2 in the psyches of all men and women.

A society based on Genesis 1, as the truth, would expect both men and women to have a career in whatever occupation or profession their talents or abilities leads them to choose.

If a couple wants to have children, caring for them physically, emotionally and financially would be the responsibility of both parents and they would both have been educated to be able to fulfil these roles. Parents who both work part-time in the workplace and part-time caring for home and children would have an enriched, more balanced life. This would not only benefit themselves, their children and the marriage but society as a whole. It could lead to greater harmony between couples and even ultimately between nations as they would no longer want to go to war.

When it is fully accepted by those who believe in the truth of the Bible that men and women were made at the same time in the image of God who is male and female then full equality would be accepted as a fact. Not only men but women would lead a rich and fulfilling life as their birthright—based on their ability, intelligence, education, and aptitude, not their gender.

It will take time for all the negative consequences of belief in the truth of Genesis 2 to be overcome and replaced by the positive messages of Genesis 1.

This is already starting to happen. It is no longer unusual for women to be in positions of power in many parts of the world. Women are increasingly respected and treated as equals in the home, at work and in their interpersonal and sexual lives in a civilised society.

No man has to sacrifice being a father in order to have a career and as men and women are increasingly recognised as being equal no woman will have to sacrifice having children, or employ another woman to care for them in order to have her own career as well.

When I was told the story of Adam and Eve I was not told that God was so angry after he had discovered Adam and Eve had eaten fruit from the tree of knowledge he told Eve he would greatly multiply her sorrow and she would bring forth children in sorrow or according to the Catholic Bible online she would bring forth her children in pain.

By the time I heard this part of the story I had already read the book by English obstetrician Dr Grantly Dick Read called "Childbirth without Fear" first published in 1956.

Dr Read says childbirth is natural and is not meant to be painful. He says in 95% of cases the pain is caused by fear and tension which activate the "fight or flight" response. This filters the blood away from the uterus into the muscles and prevents the uterus from functioning normally. Fear is what causes the pain. He says elimination of fear eliminates the pain.

For me being pregnant and giving birth to our children was the most joyous, enjoyable time of my whole life. I am very glad I was not indoctrinated into ever believing that it would be other than the memorable, fulfilling and rewarding experience that it was for me.

6

GENESIS CHAPTER 2 & 3

1 The first Sabbath 8 The garden of Eden. 17 The tree of knowledge. 21 The making of woman and institution marriage.
Thus the heavens and the earth were finished, and all the host of them.

2 And on the seventh day God ended his work which he had made: and he rested on the seventh day from all his work which he had made.

3 And God blessed the seventh day, and sanctified it: because that in it he had rested from all his work which God created and made.

4 These are the generations of the heavens and of the earth when they were created, in the day that the Lord God made the earth and the heavens.

5 And every plant of the field before it was in the earth, and every herb of the field before it grew: for the Lord God had not caused it to rain upon the earth, and there was not a man to till the ground.

6 But there went up a mist from the earth, and watered the whole face of the ground.

7 And the Lord God formed man of the dust of the ground, and breathed into his nostrils the breath of life: And man became a living soul.

8 And the Lord God planted a garden eastward in Eden: and there he put the man whom he had formed.

9 And out of the ground made the Lord God to grow every tree that is pleasant to the sight, and good for food: the tree of life also in the midst of the garden, and the tree of knowledge of good and evil.

10 And a river went out of Eden to water the garden: and from thence it was parted, and became into four heads.

11 The name of the first is Pison: that is it which compasseth the whole land of Havilah where there is gold:

12 And the gold of that land is good: there is bdellium and onyx stone.

13 And the name of the second river is Gibon: the same is it that compasseth the whole land of Ethiopia.

14 And the name of the third river is Hiddekel: that is it which goeth toward the east of Assyria. And the fourth river is Euphrates.

15 And the Lord God took the man and put him in the garden of Eden to dress it and to keep it.

16 And the Lord God commanded the man, saying, Of every tree of the garden thou mayest freely eat.

17 But of the tree of knowledge of good and evil, thou shalt not eat of it for in the day that thou eatest thereof thou shalt surely die.

18 And the Lord God said, it is not good that man should be alone; I will make him an help meet for him.

19 And out of the ground the Lord God formed every beast of the field, and every fowl of the air: and brought them unto Adam to see what he would call them: and whatsoever Adam called every living creature, that was the name thereof.

20 And Adam gave names to all the cattle, and to the fowl of the air, and to every beast of the field: but for Adam there was not found a help meet for him.

21 And the Lord God caused a deep sleep to fall upon Adam, and he slept: and he took one of his ribs, And closed up the flesh instead thereof.

22 And the rib, which the Lord God had taken from man, made he a woman, and brought her unto the man.

23 And Adam said, This is now bone of my bones, and flesh of my flesh: she shall be called Woman, because she was taken out of man.

24 Therefore shall a man leave his father and his mother, and shall cleave unto his wife: and they shall be one flesh.

25 And they were both naked, the man and his wife, and were not ashamed.

Chapter 3

1 The serpent deceiveth Eve. 6 Man's shameful fall. 14 The serpent is cursed. 15 The promised seed. 16 mankind's punishment, and loss of paradise.

Now the serpent was more subtil than any beast of the field which the lord God had made.

And he said unto the woman, Yes, hath not God said, ye shall eat of every tree of the garden?

2 And the woman said unto the serpent We may eat of the fruit of the trees of the garden:

3 But of the fruit of the tree which is in the midst of the garden, God hath said, ye shall not eat of it, neither shall ye touch it, lest ye die

4 And the serpent said unto the woman, Ye shall not surely die

5 For God doth know that in the day ye eat thereof, then your eyes shall be opened and ye shall be as gods, knowing good and evil.

6 And when the woman saw that the tree was good for food, and that it was pleasant to the eyes, and a tree to be desired to make one wise, she took of the fruit thereof, and did eat, and gave also unto her husband with her; and he did eat.

7 And the eyes of them both were opened, and they knew that they were naked: and they sewed fig leaves together and made themselves aprons.

8 And they heard the voice of the Lord God walking in the garden in the cool of the day: Adam and his wife hid themselves from the presence of the Lord God amongst the trees of the garden.

9 And the Lord God called unto Adam, and said unto him, Where art thou? And he said, I heard thy voice in the garden, and I was afraid, because I was naked; and I hid myself.

11 And he said, Who told thee that thou wast naked? Hast thou eaten of the tree, whereof commanded thee that thou shouldest not eat?

12 And the man said, The woman whom thou gavest to be with me, she gave me of the tree, and I did eat.

13 And the Lord God said unto the woman, What is this that thou hast done? And the woman said, The Serpent beguiled me, and I did eat.

14 And the Lord God said unto the serpent, Because thou hast done this, thou art cursed above all cattle, and above every beast of the field; upon thy belly shalt thou go, and dust shalt thou eat all the days of thy life:

15 And I will put enmity between thee and the woman, and between thy seed and her seed: it shall bruise thy head, and thou shalt bruise his heel.

16 Unto the woman he said, I will greatly multiply thy sorrow and thy conception; in sorrow thou shalt bring forth children; and thy desire shall be to thy husband, and he shall rule over thee.

17 And unto Adam he said, Because thou hast hearkened unto the voice of thy wife, and hast eaten of the tree, of which I commanded thee, saying, Thou shalt not eat of it: cursed is the ground for thy sake; in sorrow shalt thou eat of it all the days of your life.

18 Thorns also and thistles shall it bring forth to thee; and thou shalt eat the herb of the field

19 In the sweat of thy face shalt thou eat bread, till thou return unto the ground; for out of it wast thou taken; for dust thou art, and unto dust shalt thou return.

20 And Adam called his wife's name Eve; because she was the mother of all living.

21 Unto Adam also and to his wife did the Lord God make coats of skin and clothed them.

22 And the Lord God said, Behold, the man is become as one of us, to know good and evil and now, lest he put forth his hand, and take also of the tree of life, and eat, and live for ever,

23 Therefore the Lord God sent him forth from the garden of Eden, to till the ground from whence he was taken.

24 So he drove out the man; and he placed at the east of the garden of Eden Cherubims, and a flaming sword which turned every way to keep the way of the tree of life.

The last sentence in Genesis 1 ends with the words "And the evening and the morning were the sixth day." Genesis 2 seems to continue from Genesis 1 by commencing with the words "Thus the heavens and the earth were finished, and all the host of them."

V2 "and on the seventh day God ended his work which he had made: and he rested on the seventh day from all his work which he had made."

This gives the impression that there is only one story of the creation even though Genesis 2 goes on to give an entirely different account of the creation of man from the one in Genesis 1.

The only mention of man created in the image of God is in Genesis 1 which states:

V 27 So God created man in his image, in the image of God created he him: male and female created he them.

The Church uses the first part of V27, "so God created man in his image" and completely disregards the rest of the sentence which is "in the image of God created he him: male and female created he them."

By comparing Genesis 1 with Genesis 2 it seems clear that Genesis 1 and Genesis 2 are in fact two different stories of the Creation.

The male God in the Genesis 2 version made man from the dust of the ground and expressly commanded him not to eat from the tree of knowledge of good and evil which would have made man like God.

Clearly God did not want Man to be "in his Image" in the Adam and Eve version. Genesis 2.

V 7 "And the Lord God formed man of the dust of the ground, and breathed into his nostrils the breath of life and man became a living soul.

V 18 And the Lord God said, It is not good that the man should be alone: I will make him an help meet for him.

V 19 And out of the ground the Lord God formed every beast of the field, and every fowl of the air; and brought them unto Adam to see what he would call them: and whatsoever Adam called every living creature, that was the name thereof.

V 20 And Adam gave names to all cattle, and to the fowl of the air, and to every beast of the field; but for Adam there was no help meet for him.

In Genesis 1 God made the cattle before God made humans and in Genesis 2 God made cattle as companions for Adam—and as the cattle were not companions for him God took his rib and made the woman to be his companion and told them both they must not eat from the Tree of Knowledge.

Because they disobeyed this commandment it is written in Genesis 2, Chi. 3 V22

"And the Lord God said, Behold, the man is become as one of us, to know good and evil and now lest he put forth his hand, and take also of the tree of life, and eat, and live forever V23 therefore the Lord God sent him forth from the garden of Eden, to till the ground from whence he was taken."

I can only surmise that the Church does not recognise Genesis 1 as a separate version as it is not in the Church's interest to consider any information which would challenge the superior status of man over woman as it appears in Genesis 2.

It seems the Church wanted to keep the power and authority in the hands of the men so it would not allow the more evolved ideas in Genesis 1 to challenge the status quo at that time.

I can understand why most men seem to have no interest in the fact that Adam and Eve is not the only version of the creation in the Bible.

When I wrote in a university assignment for a General Studies Course "God made man and woman at the same time." the Professor returned my assignment with a note opposite that statement saying "No he didn't. He made Adam first."

When our eldest child was told the Adam and Eve story at school, he checked out himself, his brothers and sisters and decided it was not true, he said "because if it were true, the boys would be missing one rib."

He is now a scientist and is of the opinion that telling children this story as the truth amounts to child abuse which should be prohibited by law with which opinion I fully agree

The literal interpretation of Genesis 2 by Christian churches has caused and is still causing hatred and fear of women probably ever since it was written.

I am angry the churches have denied us the right to make our own choice as to which version, if either, of the creation stories we wish to accept.

It is in the interest of the churches to keep people ignorant of the fact that there is a choice in the Bible. This explains to me why we were told at school "Catholics are not allowed to read the Bible and have to accept on faith what they are told."

The whole of the Catholic church's teachings seems to be based on the truth of Genesis 2.

Because of Adam and Eve's disobedience, we are all born sinners and have to suffer in this world to atone for our sins. If we obey the church rules and do not break any of them then when we die we will go to heaven and live forever with Jesus.

I am angry that the story of Adam and Eve is so entrenched in peoples' psyche and is so pervasive that even those who have never read Genesis 2 accept the story as true and become negatively influenced by it. What seems urgently needed is research into the true effect of the Catholic Church's teachings on its members. There must be something wrong it is mainly the Catholic priests who are the ones who have had an ongoing history of abuse of women and children which has been systematically covered up for so many years.

The story of Adam and Eve told to children is instilling in them the idea the man is superior to woman who was only created as a companion for the man and was an evil person who caused death, pain and suffering in the world.

Even worse and more harmful is the idea because she tempted Adam to break God's Commandment not to eat fruit from the Tree of Knowledge (commonly accepted as meaning sexual knowledge) is the idea that we are born sinners because sex was prohibited by God.

Is the church telling us in order to be good humans we need to deny our sexual nature?

Did God create a man then a woman to keep him company so the two of them would live in Paradise forever if they obeyed His commandment or did God create a man and a woman to they would be fruitful and multiply and replenish the earth, and subdue it?

Were children taught the Genesis 1 version as the truth they would believe God is both male and female, men and women were created in the image of God at the same time and they were blessed by God and told to be fruitful and multiply therefore our sexual nature is God—given and a sacred part of who we are. This is the opposite of what they learn from the Genesis 2 version in which sex is sin.

The God of Genesis 2 is an angry vengeful authoritarian who cursed the snake for tempting Eve and cursed the ground from which Adam was made.

He multiplied Eve's sorrows and told her she would bring forth her children in sorrow in the King James version of the Bible. According to the Catholic Bible Online, God says to the woman "I shall give you intense pain in childbearing, you will give birth to your children in pain. Your yearning will be for your husband and he will dominate you." Both versions of the Bible punish the woman during childbirth for having had sexual intercourse which God had forbidden!

There is conflict between the God in Genesis 1 who made men and women in God's image, blessed them and told them to be fruitful and multiply and the Genesis 2 God who forbad Adam and Eve to eat fruit from the tree of knowledge of good and evil because doing so would make them like God.

How could these different stories constitute only the one creation story?

The status of women has changed since Genesis 2 was written. Is it not time for all the Christian churches to also change?

Rather than accept Genesis 1 the Sydney Anglican Diocese has reinforced Genesis 2 by changing the marriage vows so women promise to "submit" to, not obey, their husbands.

They are also required to submit to men in their churches and in the workplaces, according to Julia Baird in her article No place for spirited women (P9 S.M.Herald 27th August 2012.)

How can the ethos of the Christian churches change so women are acknowledged as equal unless they accept Genesis 1 as a separate story of equal authority to Genesis 2 and base their belief system and doctrinal teachings on this version instead of the Genesis 2 version?

It is not so long ago people believed homosexuality was a life—style choice and homosexual men were put into prison for being born different from heterosexuals and acting in the way which was natural for them to act.

I am angry the kind, loving, young brother of a fellow student at the Kindergarten Teachers College was gaoled for two years for being the homosexual he was born to be.

Although homosexuality is no longer a crime the Catholic, Anglican and most of the other established Christian churches ignore the medical evidence it is inborn and not a choice and regard homosexuality as an abnormality which offends God.

I am angry these churches ignore the effect their attitude has on society in general and on homosexual people in particular and the suicide rate among young men who are ashamed they are not only different from most of their peers but are morally unacceptable as well.

How can Christians assert man was made in the image of God and exclude homosexual men as abnormal and offensive to the God who created them?

The Catholic church does not accept sex between heterosexuals as normal and natural either unless it takes place within marriage for the purpose of having children.

The Catholic church prohibits the use of contraceptives.

Is this because of its belief in the literal truth of Genesis 2 and the need for humans to be punished for having sex—the original sin—by disallowing sex unless there is the possibility the women will suffer pain in childbirth and be dominated by their husbands?

The Catholic church is opposed to any form of euthanasia for human beings.

In the article "Euthanasia is a Bad law by Bad People says Bishop." written by Leisha Mckenny (Religious Affairs) in the Sydney Morning Herald 1st February 2011) she says the Catholic bishop of Parramatta has warned a congregation of eminent members of the legal profession at St Mary's Cathedral that legalising Euthanasia would be a bad law contrary to the ideals of justice and would corrupt society.

Could it be the Church is opposed to euthanasia because of the belief that Genesis 2 is the literal truth and the longer people have in which to suffer, the greater is the likelihood that they may repent of their past sins and be able to go to heaven when they die?

Is it not more christian and compassionate for the government to pass legislation on euthanasia in the form that is used in Oregon USA?

In an Article in the Sydney Morning Herald on the 19th August 2010 Adele Horin says the State of Oregon legislation takes control over the end of life away from doctors and gives it to the terminally ill competent persons.

Such persons are given a prescription at his or her request for medication which must be taken by the patients themselves when they decide they want to die.

Associate Professor Barbara Glidwell who was visiting Australia at the time said the law had worked well since it was passed in 1997.

The legalization of euthanasia has been discussed on the radio and on TV in Sydney and it seems that many people prefer to have the right to be able to determine whether they want to live or die for themselves and not have the matter determined by their doctors or relatives.

Once they are declared terminally ill surely they have the right to end their lives with dignity?

On what basis do the medical profession and the churches deny terminally ill people their wish to end their suffering?

Surely the "sanctity of life" does not include living in extreme pain with no quality of life, or existing in a vegetative state and being kept alive by machines?

I do not understand why assisting a person to do something which is legal (committing suicide) is a crime punishable by law.

This seems to be an unjust and unjustifiable law which causes needless suffering to the terminally ill and to their loved ones who wish to help them do what is their legal right and their wish to do and to me needs to be changed as it is unfair and unreasonable.

It seems more reasonable once two doctors have certified a person is terminally ill and wishes to die sooner rather than later that person is entitled to assistance if he or she is unable to die without help at whatever time he or she decides is the right time to do so.

The Christian churches profess to be a force for the good of mankind.

What is Christian about denying people the right to die if they are terminally ill?

For the churches to deny people the right to die with dignity is I feel religious sadism.

What is Christian about denying men and women the right to choose whether they wish to have children or not?

What is Christian about prohibiting the use of condoms to help stop the spread of Aids?

What is Christian about forbidding abortion even if the child was conceived because of incest or rape?

What is Christian about prohibiting same sex marriage if the couple is in a committed loving relationship?

In the Weekend Edition of The Sydney Morning Herald June 16-17, 2012 in News P6 is an article written by Leesha Mckenny in which she states that the leaders of the major Christian churches are united in their opposition to changes in the Marriage Act allowing same sex marriage which legislation will be debated in the lower house and will be urging their followers to write to their MPs to vote against changing the Marriage Act.

What is Christian about not allowing the Marriage Act to be changed so as to include any committed couples whether they are the same sex or of different sexes?

What is Christian about excluding women from the priesthood and treating them as evil, subservient, sex objects, to be feared, ridiculed, ruled over and used by men which are the attitudes fostered by the teaching of Genesis 2 as the truth and the only creation story in the Bible?

Why did Jesus have to die for our sins? What sins? There is no original sin in Genesis 1.

I remember being told at school that we had to offer up our suffering in order to help souls get out of Purgatory and be allowed into Heaven. Babies who had not been cleansed of original sin through Baptism had to go to Limbo instead of being allowed into heaven.

I remember visiting old and dying relatives as a child and one uncle saying to me "If you knit on a Sunday, when you die you will have to undo all the stitches with your nose."

As a child I believed everything an adult told me was true—including being punished for knitting on the Sabbath because God in Genesis 2 rested on a Sunday.

Being told the story of Adam and Eve as the truth has caused harm not only to me but to many generations of women and men.

Feeling that we have all been "hoodwinked" is the greatest source of why I am so angry.

My adopted aunt is the only adult who told me a story which was positive not negative when I was growing up. She told me the difference between heaven and hell.

She told me in both heaven and hell there was an abundance of food however it could only be eaten by the use of a very long fork. In hell everyone was trying to get the food into his or her own mouth, which was impossible, so everyone starved and suffered for all Eternity.

In heaven, everyone was focussed on feeding the other people not themselves so nobody starved and everyone was well and happy for all eternity.

My adopted Aunt had a big influence in my life. She had attended until the end of high school, an English school in Athens. She loved reading, music, opera and the theatre. She included my sister and me in many of her family outings and some of their holidays. She helped us to enjoy what she enjoyed. By buying group tickets for the theatre and for the cinema and including us she enriched our lives and ensured we had a happier and more pleasurable time during our teenage years.

When she could no longer look after herself she would say "Here are my girls" and seemed glad and happy to see us whenever my sister and I visited her at the nursing home.

She was approaching her ninetieth birthday.

Late one afternoon I had a very strong feeling I needed to go to see her.

Her younger daughter was standing by her bedside when I entered the room.

She told me her mother had stopped eating, drinking, speaking or getting out of bed.

Her mother looked very small curled up in the bed with her eyes closed.

I felt I needed to do something so I said to her "Your husband and my mother and father are waiting for you in Heaven Aunty"

I don't know whether she heard me or if she had whether she believed me.

I was told she died peacefully later that evening.

She had helped me to live and I trust I had helped her to die by giving her hope whether it was based on the truth or not.

Belief in life after death can have positive effects as well as negative ones. Even belief in hell may have helped keep some people stay on the straight and narrow path through fear.

My being told the Story of Adam and Eve as the truth however had a completely negative effect on me and did not benefit me in any way as far as I am aware.

I remember being told as a child, that Jewish boys every night in their prayers say "Thank you God for not having made me a woman,"

I wonder if this is true and whether the Jewish girls thank God every night for not having made them men?

I am not angry about religious ideas even if they are not evidence based which give some people hope while not causing harm to other people.

I am angry about the story of Adam and Eve being told as being literally true and the negative effect it has had on all women.

I am angry about the Edict of 1377 which was a direct result of the belief in the literal truth of the Adam and Eve Genesis 2 version of the creation banning women from going to the University of Bologna and having such a lasting devastating effect on women.

I wish it were true that nobody believes in the literal truth of the story of Adam and Eve these days.

I am angry at the amount of evidence in the community that the attitudes engendered by belief in the literal truth of the story of Adam and Eve are still very much in existence especially in the Catholic and Greek Orthodox churches.

During my search for the truth I found an article which states that all cultures have creation myths, typically in multiple versions. They tell us how the world and human life came into existence. These myths are the basis of how people relate to the natural world and each other and reveal our real prejudices and our real priorities. I believe the Christian churches, whether they teach Adam and Eve as the literal truth or as symbolic, by not acknowledging the separate existence of Genesis 1— are revealing their real prejudice against women and their real priority, the superiority of men. Because of my personal experience I am very angry the church view seems to be generally accepted without challenge by people who have never heard of Genesis 1 and I feel it is time for this to be changed.

My parent's engagement photo from which I can
see I did not inherit the slim gene.

7

OVERCOMING MY EATING PROBLEM

OVER THE PAST FEW YEARS I have been giving a lot of attention to the "inside" Helen and have found shameful feelings of failure and considerable anger over loss of my dreams.

In my attempt to help the child Helen to "grow up" I have looked back on why I am so angry and have found that underneath what I thought was anger was a feeling of being hurt or of feeling excluded because I felt different.

What seemed so important at the time has now become less important and I need to put it all behind me and forgive and forget most of it.

I have read and re-read the report from the good psychologist and I feel I have changed my belief system and am no longer so controlled by what I was told at school and at home.

I no longer believe that life is about suffering to atone for the sin of Adam and Eve which I no longer believe is the literal truth but is a religious myth.

I feel I have successfully confronted the assumptions of the Catholic Faith at that time so they have lost their restricting power over me.

I do not accept I need to develop a psychological part which will be my own best friend as I am an introvert and have always been my own best friend.

I have always accepted my inner self.

It is my exterior self I did not and have not yet fully accepted and I feel I can not accept until I look more like I looked when I was working outside the home for the three years and felt happier and more fulfilled.

Until a few years ago I thought I had overcome my addiction to carbohydrates.

I had been eating high protein and low carbohydrate food for several weeks and my clothes were feeling more comfortable.

On this particular morning I woke up early and couldn't go back to sleep. The weather had been cold and miserable for two days. The previous day I had stayed home typing on my computer. I felt sleep deprived and craved milk chocolate.

I had scrambled egg with ricotta and chicken for breakfast and I still craved milk chocolate.

I rang my sister to see how the surprise party for a woman we both knew had been and she said she would ring me back that night as she was going to Bridge.

I decided I needed to get out of the house and do some walking.

It was still cold, wet, grey and miserable.

Jim said he would come for a bus ride to the shopping centre with me and would have a cup of coffee while I looked for bargains at the sales most of the shops were having.

It had been some weeks since I had been to a seminar where I had been given names of organizations which use volunteer counsellors and I wanted to get down to goal weight and buy some new clothes before I made any enquiries and applications.

The football season was taking its toll on me as Jim watches the Rugby games on Friday and Saturday evenings at the Club or at home and spends the rest of the time reading about or talking about the performances or watching the videos of them for hours at a time.

Rugby seems to be his all encompassing passion and leaves me unreasonably angry and irritable as I feel totally excluded.

On the way to and in the shopping centre I still craved milk chocolate.

I looked in some of the shops while Jim had his coffee. I found nothing of interest and I still craved milk chocolate.

When we went to one of the supermarkets I was delighted to find that they had a sale on chocolates so I bought a bag of fifteen small bars of milk chocolate and two large 175g blocks of milk chocolate. In the bus back on the way home I could hardly wait to eat as much of the chocolate as I could. The more I ate the more I wanted to eat. I bought two more 100g milk chocolate blocks with peppermint filling at the local supermarket before I went home.

Normally I don't eat while I am on the bus and normally I find milk chocolate sickly sweet and prefer dark chocolate.

I had not had a chocolate binge of that magnitude since I was a teenager and I wanted to understand what had triggered it.

I always look for possible psychological reasons first and now I am aware that there could be physiological or genetic reasons in addition to or instead of the psychological ones. I looked up "Causes of Eating Disorders" on the Internet and found an interesting article which I found very helpful.

I did not feel sorry about eating the chocolate though I felt uncomfortable and unhappy as my clothes felt tighter and I felt at least five kilos heavier.

I felt quite hopeless and felt I would never achieve my goal of my being within the normal BMI range for a woman and be able to buy clothes I liked to wear. I felt I would never be the size I was meant to be.

I thought back and tried to remember everything that had happened and how I had felt on that day and the day before the craving had started.

The first thing I remembered was my sister's telling me she had been invited to attend the surprise birthday party being given by the children of a woman we had both known since our Youth Club days. My sister had maintained the friendship with her and I had not, so I did not expect an invitation however I was reminded that my sister had always been more accepted and popular than I had ever been. I know this had more to do with my attitude rather than my size as there was one girl in our Youth Club who was taller and larger than I was. She went swimming while I would never be seen in a swim suit. She appeared to be self confident and happy, out-going, friendly and gregarious. I was either genetically the opposite or had become so due to the home and school environment in which I was growing up I feel.

In the Greek culture at that time we did not usually celebrate individual birthdays.

Everybody went to parties for people who shared the same saint's christian name.

I do not remember having a birthday party myself or going to anyone else's birthday party except once in primary school and then when I turned thirteen I was allowed to ask some girls from school to come to our home for a party.

This was not a happy occasion as none of the girls ate any of the Greek sweets my mother had made and my party made me feel even more different and unacceptable.

I am angry that a few days later an older boy in the neighbourhood saw my sister and me outside our house as he was walking past and called out to us "Why don't you go back to where you came from?" We were born in Sydney so I was not hurt however I remembered being on the tram with my mother and father who were talking to each other in Greek and a man angrily shouting "Speak English!" to them and that did upset me.

I had been keeping my promise to myself not to eat bread, rice, chocolate, any sugar, fruit, nuts, mixed seeds and vegetables and I was happy about that however I was disappointed to find after the six weeks my weight had stayed the same!

It was still cold, wet, grey and miserable and I had woken at 5 am and couldn't sleep again.

Jim had been looking "off colour" for several days and complained of feeling quite unwell.

He had not slept well or eaten well ever since we had been given an old ornamental Chinese bowl which I liked and he very much disliked.

He particularly disliked it as he believed it was bad luck to be given anything Chinese by a person who was not Chinese as was the case with this bowl.

He had not told me how he felt about it until the day of the binge.

We have agreed that if ever there was a disagreement between us that involved how each of us felt about something we would both go along with whichever of us had the stronger feeling about it.

When we put the bowl in the bottom of a cupboard with the intention of getting rid of it as soon as possible he immediately returned to normal.

This further convinced me of the power of the mind about which I had learned while I was at the Sydney Kindergarten Teachers Training College. It was there I learned, for the first time what a person believes to be the truth influences how that person feels and how that person behaves even if what they believe to be the truth is in fact not the truth but a lie.

After my chocolate binge I kept eating bread, fruit, vegetables, nuts and everything else of which I had deprived myself for six weeks until I felt I had had enough.

Even though I had remained the same weight and had had a binge I had proven to myself that I could do it. I was happy I had made a plan and I had managed to stick to it.

It reminded me of the time I went to a Health Farm and lived on water for seven days.

I lost only one pound, developed a cyst which had to be surgically removed from my eyelid and a very bad cold which stayed with me for the next three months.

In spite of this I am glad I did it and have a certificate to prove that I did.

After five days of unrestricted eating I regained my hope I would eventually reach my goal by doing things very differently from now on.

I am angry at the number of times I have found myself exactly in this same position.

I follow a path enthusiastically only to find I have been on the wrong path.

I seem to be a very slow learner and I wonder what is stopping me from changing my behaviour and becoming the person I want to be?

I searched the Internet and found another article which was very helpful as I could see immediately that I fitted the profile of a person with a Binge Eating Disorder.

I am angry that in all the years of my seeking professional help regarding my problem with food not one person other than the good psychologist mentioned my having a binge eating disorder.

This article is at http://helpguide.org/mental/binge_eating_disorder.htm

From reading the articles on the internet I learned information which I feel "speaks" to me.

From this article I learned that if you compulsively overeat food, are out of control and can't stop on a regular basis you have a binge eating disorder.

This is what I have been doing ever since I can remember.

Wanting to stop and being unable to stop and not knowing what triggers the binge in the first place was the worst part of it.

I feel angry with myself and feel inadequate and inferior to people who succeed in reaching their goal weight whenever they decide to do so and I can't.

I identify completely with all the following symptoms all of which I feel apply to me.

EMOTIONAL SYMPTOMS

Never feeling satisfied, no matter how much you eat.
Feeling guilty or depressed after over-eating.

BIOLOGICAL CAUSES

Under this heading it was said that the hypothalamus which controls the appetite may not be sending correct messages about hunger and fullness and that it has been found by researchers that a genetic mutation appears to cause food addiction.

There is evidence, also, that low levels of the brain chemical, serotonin play a role in compulsive eating.

Recently through the screening of brain scans it has been found there is a difference between the obese and average weight people in their levels of hunger. The brains of the obese do not register as high levels of hunger or satisfaction as the normal brains do,

SOCIAL AND CULTURAL CAUSES.

Social pressure to be thin can increase the incidence of emotional eating. Some parents unknowingly can cause future binge eating by giving their children food to reward or comfort them or just to keep them quiet.

Always commenting on their appearance can make their children vulnerable.

Whether I was up or down in weight was always commented on by my relatives and friends much to my annoyance and embarrassment.

Now I say "I have always gone up and down in weight and I prefer you do not comment on it as it upsets me."

PSYCHOLOGICAL CAUSES

Binge eating may be due to a person either suffering from depression or having been recently depressed.

Binge eating can also be caused by a person's having poor impulse control or needing to repress or suppress uncomfortable feelings.

Having low self esteem and not liking one's body or how one looks can also trigger a binge eating attack.

I know now I was depressed and that is why I put on so much weight by the time I left school.

I also know I still suffer from low self-esteem and body dissatisfaction which I feel will improve only when I achieve my personal goal weight.

STRESS

One of the most common reasons for compulsive eating is to relieve stress and suppress one's unpleasant emotions.

Binge eating can make feelings such as stress, sadness, depression, anxiety and boredom disappear even if only for a short time.

I have found personally that by giving myself permission to eat any type of food whenever I feel like eating it prevents my having a binge later most of the time.

Of the 10 Strategies listed for Overcoming Binge Eating the three which appeal most to me are:

(1) Avoid temptation by removing all the binge foods from your home.
(2) Stop Dieting as deprivation and hunger can trigger food craving.
(3) Exercise as it lifts depression, reduces stress and helps stop Emotional Eating.

From the article on What Causes Eating Disorders I learned that there is never only one single cause for an Eating disorder.

An eating disorder can arise because of a combination of physical, emotional, psychological, relational or sociological conditions of long standing.

I can relate to the following statements made in the article.

People with eating disorders often use food in an attempt to compensate for feelings and emotions with which they are unable to cope.

Sometimes an eating disorder can be an unconscious reaction to make up for past childhood abuse or trauma, problems in one's family or mistakes one has made in the past.

An eating disorder can become an explanation and reason justifying the lack of a happy and satisfying life.

An eating disorder can be an indirect way of communication about pain and suffering.

Common triggers can be changes in the environment, moving from home or school or trauma of any sort. I found this particularly interesting as all of these things had happened to me. Most patients with eating disorders are affected by little traumas not necessarily big traumas.

People prone to eating disorders seem to be more sensitive individuals.

These last two statements explain why some children are adversely affected by the Adam and Eve story while most children are not.

I am not qualified to determine what caused me to develop an eating disorder.

I suspect that my going to that school and everything that happened while I was there had a great deal to do with my developing an eating disorder.

In my mind the trauma of my being told the story of Adam and Eve as fact and my believing everything I had been told was one of the most important factors which led to my abnormal eating habits.

I am angry about this and I am finding it difficult to let it go as I firmly believe it was being told the story of Adam and Eve as the truth which was the trauma which triggered my overeating reaction and caused food to become my enemy and eating became a sin.

I know I need to overcome my early conditioning and change my attitude to food. I feel it will not be easy to no longer think of eating as sinful and any food as forbidden and become a normal eater who loves and enjoys eating food which is nutritious and satisfying.

I can relate to the following statements made in the What is an Eating Disorder article.

Eating disorders are a false form of communication about pain and suffering and the person needs to be more direct with himself or herself and with other people.

An eating disorder can be a false form of comfort and safety by relieving anxiety and avoiding painful emotions.

An eating disorder can give a false sense of being special or unique and healing can start when there are no special rules or requirements for them different from other people.

An eating disorder can be a false pursuit of perfection by the feeling that if one improves one's body it will make up for one's other perceived inadequacies and failures.

An eating disorder can be false compensation for the past childhood abuse or trauma.

Letting go of the past is a process in which one accepts the past cannot be changed and one concentrates on the present and the future.

I no longer automatically put food into my mouth when I am feeling stressed.

Sometimes my urge to eat becomes imperative and I can not stop even though I know the consequences of not doing so.

I thought this was a psychological weakness in me and I now know it happens when my blood pressure goes up in response to my eating too much salt.

I have only recently made this connection and I wonder if this has always been the case.

When I am in this state I can't divert myself from eating whereas at other times I can.

By having checked my blood pressure before and after a binge I have on two occasions found a drop in my systolic pressure of over thirty degrees after the binge.

When the children were all living at home and I had no help I used to divert myself from eating by spending many hours tiling the back patio.

I also enjoyed making a mosaic panel on the left side of the front door and putting ceramic tiles on all the flat surfaces I could find inside the house.

I did quite a few paintings many of which I threw away and some of which I have kept and have on some of the walls in our unit.

Now I enjoy using fabric paint to change the look of various items of my clothing, some of which I keep and some of which go into the clothing bin.

I have found the best way to avoid over-eating is to get out of the house and walk or go to a class or workshop or on a bus or train ride to another suburb.

I usually resort to binge eating to relieve boredom when I am at home and I do not feel the urge to over-eat when I am out of the house.

I remember as a child praying it would not rain as my mother always cancelled any planned outing if it was raining.

My having to stay home was often used by my mother as a threat to stop my doing anything I was doing of which she did not approve.

I am angry she treated staying home as a punishment.

Until recently my staying home caused me to automatically eat carbohydrates to comfort myself and relieve the stressful feelings the origin of which I was unaware.

It has taken me a long time to realise as an adult I have the right to make my own choices.

I no longer have to adhere to the family and school rules or to be so accommodating.

I am now free to go out whenever I choose, eat whatever I want to eat, wear whatever I want to wear and do whatever I would like to do as long as it is legal.

I know how I look is completely insignificant on the universal scale of what matters however it still matters to me.

I am not free to do whatever I would like to do because I am not happy with the way I look.

I had been the fattest girl in the school and I was usually the fattest person in the street. I felt my fat protected me from the male gaze and the evil eye and kept me safe even though I disliked it and was always consciously trying to get rid of it.

My subconscious refused to allow this to happen until I felt I was in a safe environment such as when I went to work outside the home for three years, with like-minded people.

I knew after spending so much time looking at the "Inside Helen" and helping her to grow-up, making all the changes suggested in the report by the good psychologist, writing down why I am so angry and connecting with my anger, there was still more I needed to do or that needed to happen before I could really change myself.

In May 2011, I attended a Two Day Workshop by a visiting American Psychologist, Dr John B. Arden and also bought his book "Rewire your Brain. Think Your Way To A Better Life" (John Wiley & sons Inc. Hoboken, New Jersey 2010.)

I found the workshop stimulating and his book very easy to read. It was helpful and hope-inspiring in that it stated that the brain can grow and change with age and if you change your brain you can change your life. On the back cover of the book it says that once thought to be hard-wired the brain is actually soft-wired by experience so it is possible to rewire parts of the brain and improve your quality of life by changing what you do.

Dr Arden says in his Preface that Rewire Your Brain is meant to be a practical resource book for the general public and tells people how to go about changing their brain.

Dr Arden outlines how to go about doing that in different chapters of the book by describing new developments in Neuroscience and how they need to be applied.

Chapter five—Fueling Your Brain is about food and how what you eat affects the function and biochemistry of the brain. He suggests eating three or four well balanced meals a day and avoiding sugar and all other simple carbohydrates is best for your brain, your energy level and your general health and wellbeing.

I found this chapter a helpful guide to my making better choices regarding what to eat. A big part of my problem with food came from my mother who when she was growing up was aware though her own family had enough food to eat other people in the same neighbourhood had died and were dying of starvation because of the war.

I had not seen my mother enjoy eating and I grew up with the feeling that enjoying eating is not acceptable.

Even now when I see people eating and seemingly enjoying what they are eating I feel they are doing something wrong.

I know I need to overcome negative conditioning from both my mother and school before I can put Dr Arden's guidelines into practice and allow myself to enjoy eating nutritious food.

Chapter 7 of the book is also of particular interest to me as in it he refers to recent research which shows people who maintain positive social relationships live longer and feel more satisfied with their lives.

I usually avoid taking part in any group social gatherings. Dr Arden says to rewire our brain we need to do what we previously avoided doing and force ourselves to do what we do not really want to do.

I am not a confident out-going person and as I do not drink I do not enjoy going to a pub or being with people who like beer or wine so I am finding it hard to find a group in which I feel at home. I felt at home when I was working. This was good for me however it was not good for the younger children who were aged twelve, fourteen and seventeen.

As the older children were still living at home I thought the younger ones would be alright at home after school without adult supervision until we came home about six thirty.

I needed some "me" time and felt it had to be then or never.

I felt angry other women used their qualifications by getting a job and I was unable to do anything with my pieces of paper, except feel grateful I had them.

I am glad I took the opportunity to feel and act like a normal human by not being confined to the home for those three years. It was a totally new world for me.

I enjoyed feeling how I had imagined a normal woman would feel.

I enjoyed the male attention in what felt like a safe environment, even though on two occasions I feel I could have had an affair had I been so inclined.

The first time I was propositioned I was at a weekend conference in a hotel in Tasmania.

I was glad to see a former lecturer of mine as I was going into the conference dinner.

He walked with me into the dining room and sat with me at the end of one of the long tables which seated about twelve people. After dinner, during a lull in our conversation, he said in a loud voice "You are not really going to leave me are you Helen?"

Everyone at the table looked at us and he said to the group "We have two beautiful children and now she wants to leave me."

The music started and the woman sitting opposite us said to me, "Your husband wants to dance with you" and I replied, "He is not my husband" as he led me onto the dance floor.

I enjoyed dancing with him and as we were returning to the table he said "Your room or mine?" I took two bottles of wine from our table and he followed me to the next table where friends of his were seated. I put the bottles on the table in front of a vacant chair on which he sat and said "Good night" to everyone and left.

On the second occasion I was at a Saturday all day seminar at a hotel in North Sydney.

When the seminar ended a man I knew offered me a lift and suggested having a cup of coffee. He drank his coffee and I had half finished mine when he lent across, took my cup and drank what was left of my coffee. When we got back into the car he turned on the radio which was playing Richard Tauber singing "'Girls were made to love and kiss", kissed me and said "What a lovely way to end a seminar!

We are both adults. What about coming back to the office with me?"

I told him I was running late and was expected home so would he please take me to the station and he did.

I am very grateful to him for the new feelings he had aroused in me.

I am angry these two incidents were the most romantic, exciting, memorable encounters with men I had ever had in my life.

In the Greek community it would have been considered disgraceful for a married woman to have been allowed to have been in the situations in which I found myself at that time.

I appreciate how much freedom I had because of the enlightened attitude of my husband.

The good psychologist was right when she wrote in her report that in the world of work, I was no longer cloistered from my own and other people's attention or desires.

Where I feel she is wrong is in going on to say that getting out of the workforce was my way of avoiding other issues this provoked.

At least consciously that is not why I left the workforce.

I knew my being in the workforce was not good for the younger children as they were not doing as well at school and I blame myself for that.

Had I known they were not old enough to be left on their own I could have made sure an adult was there when they came home from school.

I felt even worse about this when Jim told me he would have been very happy to have left work two hours earlier to be home with them. He was working a ten hour day and could easily have arranged for someone else to have closed the pharmacy had we known the children needed adult supervision.

I feel not having an adult in charge adversely affected all three of the younger children.

I feel both the girls have never forgiven me for having abandoned them during that time.

I am grateful and feel indebted to my father for his financial support as I know I could not have lived the way I lived without his financial assistance.

I am angry because I was never a permanent part of the workforce able to earn my own money and be financially independent.

I appreciate all our daughters including the two I had inadvertently abandoned have been able to do what I was not able to do.

To me this is a sign of progress and a big step forward in the area of equality of opportunity for boys and girls which was lacking when I was growing up.

I am angry both my sister and I were so restricted in what we could do and I am amazed at what Greek Australian women are able to accomplish today. A good example is Anita, my only God-child who studied law when her children were young, qualified and was admitted as a solicitor. She not only practises law she is a keen ballroom dancer who has won many awards over the years and in the most recent competition came first in the best routine section and won gold for the rest of the dances. She is now still practising law and practising for the next Ballroom Dancing Competition.

Last year after I had attended Dr Arden's Seminar I was sent a brochure which listed many therapy DVD's available for purchase.

There was one DVD," Cognitive Therapy for Weight Loss. A Coaching Session by Judith Beck. PhD." which immediately attracted my attention.

What I learned from watching this DVD, supplemented what I learned from reading Dr John Arden's Book, Rewire your Brain. Think your way to a Better Life.

Both emphasise the importance of cognition and the learning of new skills and habits in order to be able to change your brain and become the person you want to be.

Dr Judith Beck is the Director of The Beck Institute for Cognitive Therapy and Research.

She is an expert in her field and has written text books and books for the public, one of which is "the Beck DIET solution" (Robinson London 2008) which I ordered.

The DVD is of a coaching session of a patient with a food management problem.

What Dr Beck tells her patient almost immediately is that it is not her fault she could not lose weight and keep it off, because she was not taught the skills she needed to have.

She suggests to her patient, before she even attempts to change her eating habits she needs to master the necessary skills some of which are the following:

Establish good lifestyle habits such as always sitting down to eat.

Eat slowly and enjoy every mouthful.

Feel good about yourself along the way without waiting until you have lost weight to do what you would like to do.

Get better by making small changes and accept that as we are human we will all make mistakes and get back on track as soon as possible.

Everyone has to individually work out what works best for herself or himself.

Dr Beck says some people master the skills quickly and some take weeks or even months.

She said she had a personal interest in Weight Loss because from the age of sixteen her weight kept going up and down by about ten to fifteen pounds.

It was only when she applied the principles of Cognitive Therapy to her situation that she could change her behaviour, overcome the profound sense of hopelessness which she says is felt by most people with eating problems, and lead a more fulfilling life by being able to control her eating.

It took nearly a month for the Beck Diet Solution book to arrive.

I had been following most of Dr Beck's suggestions and they were not working for me.

Though I agreed with Dr Beck intellectually I found myself rebelling emotionally as I usually do as I have not yet healed the split between what I think and what I feel.

When I had read to page 37 of the book I found a questionnaire under the heading:

"Could you have an eating disorder?"

"Do you have a continuous obsession with food, dieting, weight, or appearance to the exclusion of more important aspects of your life?"

At the end of the list of questions was the statement "If you have answered yes to any of these questions, please make an appointment with a mental-health professional. This program is not suitable for you."

I felt both disappointed and relieved.

Once again I had come to the road sign "Go back. You are going the Wrong Way"

I realised I would have to find a different road or a different way of getting to my goal.

Some doctors are now advising people that as they get older it is better to be a little over what is a normal BMI than within the normal limits.

This does not change how I feel about my having a normal BMI and how I feel about my body image however it changes objectively the importance of the BMI and my attitude to what I allow myself to eat or forbid myself from eating.

Now when I eat chocolate, I don't feel hopelessly condemned to being overweight for the rest of my life. I know I will have had enough chocolate after a certain time and stop eating it.

Having both resisted and given in to my cravings I have found it is better to eat what I feel like eating at the time rather than make up for resisting by eating much more of what I had wanted later.

I empathised with a friend who told me she had resisted a slice of pavlova at the afternoon tea then bought a whole pavlova and ate all of it as soon as she got home.

I feel angry and embarrassed when I remember one afternoon tea with my mother at my aunt's house when I was eighteen. Just as the hostess was serving the pavlova my mother called out in a loud voice "None for Helen."

The best way I feel to avoid my having a binge is to give myself permission to eat what I want whenever I feel like eating it.

From now on regarding food "Anything Goes" except for the three white poisons, Sugar, White flour and Salt about which a naturopath at the Health Farm warned me many years ago and about which science is increasingly warning people today.

In the report given to me by the good psychologist she said I am a person who has been struggling with the effects of yo-yo dieting, binge eating and a tendency to adopt or try out any weight loss program which offered me a resolution of this problem.

Sixteen years have passed since then and to my dismay I find I still have the same tendency, hence my eagerly awaiting the arrival of the Beck Diet Solution Book.

I know I need to completely change my whole approach to food, eating, losing weight and how I feel about my body.

I need to listen to my inner self and be guided by my knowledge and my own experience.

As I know I respond to carbohydrates like an alcoholic does to alcohol, I need to keep that in mind when making my food choices and avoid sugar in any form as best I can.

My reading Dr Atkins Diet Revolution by Robert C Atkins MD Completely Revised Avon Books USA 2002 and Dr Atkins New Carbohydrate Gram Counter M.Evans and Company,inc.1996 is what I found most helpful in my losing the initial twenty kilos.

What I found most helpful in my search for the truth during my inner journey has been:

(1) Dr John Arden's Workshop and reading his book Rewire your Brain.

(2) Dr Judith Beck's DVD Cognitive Therapy for Weightless.

(3) http://helpguide.org/mental/binge_eating_disorder.htm

(4) Dr Susan Albers, PsyD. 50 Ways to Soothe yourself without Food. (2009) and

(5) Sunny Sea Gold food; the good girl's drug How to Stop Using Food to Control Your Feelings 2011 Berkly Books New York

To help myself further, I looked up the definition of Introvert on the Internet.

This definition is in About.com. Gifted Children

Introvert by Carol Bainbridge, About. com Guide. in which she points out although most people think introverts are just people who are shy in fact this is not the case.

Introversion is not simply shyness. Introverts are persons who derive their energy from being alone and who find being around other people very draining of their energy.

Introverts enjoy being alone and having time to think and be in touch with the inner world of their thoughts and feelings. They are not comfortable in and avoid social situations even if they have good social skills, as they need time alone more than they need to be with other people which they find very demanding and exhausting.

They enjoy the inner world of the mind and exploring their own thoughts and feelings and need some time alone after being with other people in order to be able to keep going.

Carol Bainbridge says introverts wanting to be alone is not of itself a sign of depression as either they feel they need time away from people in order to be able to regain their energy or they need time alone with their own thoughts to be quietly introspective.

Being introspective does not mean that an introvert never has conversations. However those conversations are generally about ideas and information they find interesting rather than what they consider boring social small talk.

Carol Bainbridge finally states Introverts make up only 25% to 40% of the general population however they make up 60% of the gifted population which I found intriguing.

I did not know I felt different from most people because I was in fact different from most people until I attended a weekend course called "Exploit your Potential" conducted by two psychologists for the Centre for Continuing Education at The University of Sydney in 1997. We completed a Myers Briggs questionnaire and it was then I found out I was an introvert. I identified with everything said about introverts in the definition of an introvert.

This has been very helpful because I now know I am not alone and there are many people who feel and act as I do. I know introverts are inherently different from extroverts in many ways. Being different does not mean introverts are abnormal though they may appear strange and abnormal to extroverts who are in the majority.

I have found most introverts I know understand extroverts (and some may even wish they were more like them) however the extroverts with whom I associate especially my sister not only do not understand introverts they show no interest whatsoever in doing so.

I gave my sister some information about introverts so she would stop expecting me to be like her and it made no difference to her attitude. After I had given her the information she said to me in the presence of other people "You used to invite us to dinner and then you would disappear."

I am angry because I feel had she read the information I had given her she would not have made that comment as she would have understood why I had to disappear for a while as I found cooking dinner for other people extremely stressful then and I still find it stressful now.

EPILOGUE

I HAVE RE-EVALUATED MY LIST of reasons for wanting to lose weight and there are three reasons on which I feel I need to comment.

(1) So I feel equal to all the women with whom I grew up including my sister.

I feel losing five kilos is a realistic goal however I no longer accept how much I weigh as the sole criterion on which my own self esteem and the esteem of others needs to be based. I don't need to look like all the other women physically or have the same values as they have in order to like and accept myself.

We were all born with different temperaments, abilities and attributes, so everyone of us is different. That is just how it is therefore it is OK for me to be and feel different from them. According to Genesis 1 men and women are inherently equal so why are most women and not most men judged predominantly on their appearance?

(2) So I become the shape and size I was born to be.

On my reaching puberty my mother would not buy me a brassiere. I had to wear a binder she had made for me instead. As a result I will never be the shape I was born and meant to be. I did not wear a proper bra until I had left school.

At that stage the wife of the Greek Consul who was kind and very influential in the Greek Community intervened on my behalf.

She told my mother to take me to Madame Finney who custom-made undergarments for women who were not average in size. When I took off everything from the waist up so Madame could measure me, I heard her say to my mother "What you have done is Criminal!" not realising when my mother was growing up, the flat chested boyish look was the fashion she still followed with me.

Until I connected with my feelings, I did not realise this could also be why I am and feel so different from other women I knew, especially my sister.

After I recently accompanied two friends to their medical appointments, I am now glad I am smaller in bust size than their DD size whether it is genetic or whether it is because of my mother.

(3) So I like and fully accept my body and the fact I am a sexual being.

At school we wore a below the knee dark navy uniform with black stockings and a hat and gloves and no jewellery or make-up.

The nuns told us both directly and indirectly to look attractive was sinful and dangerous.

At home the message was if we looked attractive we could be harmed by the "The Evil Eye."

There was no formal sex education at school and no formal sex education at home either.

I feel angry that when I tried to get my mother to discuss with me a book on sex I had bought, she not only refused to do so, she was very upset and in tears when she said to my sister "Do you know what sort of books your sister is reading?"

After I had also been told the Story of Adam and Eve as the truth which was the strongest of all the negative messages I had been given about women, how could I possibly have developed a more positive attitude to the fact I was born female and a sexual being?

Even though I know I would not be who I am had I not attended a Catholic school, been born an introvert and had the same parents I am angry I do not feel I am who I was born to be and I feel cheated.

I am angry because even though I may change my brain and my future I cannot change the past and make up for what I feel was negative conditioning resulting in needless suffering and unnecessary deprivation.

My mother was a true believer in the Greek Orthodox religion which is so similar to that of the Catholic religion girls at school who had to go to Mass at least once a week were told if they could not find a Catholic church it was permissible for them to attend a Greek Orthodox church instead. As both religions believe in the literal truth of the Adam and Eve version of the creation what else can they be than Anti-sex, Anti-women and Anti-enjoyment of life on earth?

The Greek Orthodox church has more elaborate dress for their priests and there are Icons on the walls of their churches. Greek priests are allowed to marry however they remain priests and are not able to progress to any higher status if they do marry.

To my knowledge there are no Greek women priests although in spite of the opposition of the Vatican it has been reported there are about one hundred and fifty Roman Catholic women priests in America.

Despite differences the basic message from both churches is the same.

We are all sinners because of Eve's disobedience and women are the source of all evil.

Is it not time to change this message to what is appropriate in the 21st Century?

On the 17th November 2011, the President of the United States, President Obama, the first American President of African American descent, was welcomed to the Australian Parliament by the first Woman Prime Minister of Australia Julia Gillard.

Women today are free to become the people they were born to be.

This is evident in the universities, in every profession, occupation, business and in every arena in which reality is demonstrating the truth of equality as it is in the Genesis 1 wherever in the world equality of opportunity for women exists.

In spite of this Christian churches are ignoring Genesis 1 and are adhering to Genesis 2 which reflected reality when it was written and not as it is in the twenty first century.

In view of this fact I do not feel that my drawing attention to the existence of Genesis 1 is or has been a complete waste of time even if my belief is proved to be wrong or without foundation and I am the only one who thinks it is so important.

Whenever or wherever I have mentioned its existence in a workshop or in an assignment nobody has discussed it with me and nobody has given me a positive response or shown any interest except our first born Denny and his partner Ann.

I have not told any of our daughters about my writing a book as when I mentioned what I was thinking to one of them her response was negative.

Our second son Michael is still of the opinion that nobody believes in the literal truth of the Adam and Eve story these days so I have been wasting my time.

Jim told me that my going on about Adam and Eve is completely useless as true believers are not going to take any notice of what I have written and no one else could care less about what is written in the Bible.

He also said "In any case I am unhappy about your book and at the way you have portrayed me as you have been very unfair."

I replied "I wrote why I am so angry from my perspective of the facts. Why don't you write your own book and give your version?"

As this did not appeal to him I suggested he write down how I have been unfair to him and I would type what he writes and include it in the Epilogue of my book.

The following is what he wrote:

"'Helen portrays me as being uncaring but she did not stop to think of my situation at the time. I had bought my own Pharmacy and for the first time I was alone with none of the support and companionship I had previously enjoyed with my family.

I had borrowed money from the bank to complete the purchase of the pharmacy and had a mortgage on the house on which my father had paid the deposit.

I was working in an unfamiliar suburb and my father was ill and was later diagnosed with inoperable cancer and died in December of that year.

The fact I was married is what added to my burden.

I have always had to work hard. I had started working at the family restaurant when I was ten years old and over the years graduated to dishwasher, floor scrubber, waiter, kitchen hand and manager of general duties involved with running a restaurant.

As a pharmacy apprentice I also had to sweep the floor, clean the windows and wash bottles.

Throughout my long working career I was in contact with many people from all walks of life whereas Helen had led a much more cloistered kind of life.

I had gone to Sydney to study at University because my elder sister was married and lived in Sydney and I could stay with her while I was studying. This is when I first met Helen as she was the cousin of my brother-in-law.

The Greek community in Wellington consisted of about two hundred and fifty people and we all knew each other. All the Greek families were on the same social level whereas in Sydney the Greek community numbered several thousands and were divided into many social groups as in any large community—rich, poor, trustworthy and untrustworthy and they seemed to associate only with the Greeks who had come from the same part or island of Greece, unlike how it was in Wellington.

That year in Sydney was the worst year of my whole life. The only thing good about it was my meeting Helen and I saw her from time to time.

At University I used to go to the movies alone and eat alone as the other students seemed to keep to groups of people with whom they had gone to school.

I missed home and though I am not a partygoer, I missed the festive occasions when every Greek in Wellington would celebrate at The Pan Hellenic Club.

When I returned to Sydney as a qualified pharmacist five years later, I was pressured to get married. I disregarded all the matchmaking and what my brother in law had told me and I did what I wanted to do and that was to ask Helen to marry me.

Her attributes were not of a practical life type like mine.

She was an enthusiastic social dancer, a singer of both classical and popular songs, a talented pianist and a qualified teacher of kindergarten children—none of which were of help to me in the practical business world in which I was living.

In spite of our differences we managed to work on issues satisfactorily all during our long marriage, perhaps because of the fact we were different and we complemented each other. I felt my actions in the early years of our marriage, which caused her to feel angry, needed to be looked at in the context of my situation at that time. Now having put my side of the story I feel a lot better about her book."

Though he feels better about my book he told me he still thinks that my writing it has been a total waste of time. As regards the public he may well be right.

As regards how it is from my point of view he is completely one hundred per cent wrong.

I was told I needed to pay attention to the inside Helen as she may be still a little girl whom I needed to help grow up and this is what I did.

I looked up "to grow up" on the internet and I found a very interesting essay written by Dr Gerard Stein—Blogging about Psychotherapy from Chicago. Signs of Maturity: What does it mean to "Grow Up?"

Of the signs of maturity to which he refers I feel I already achieved some and am in the process of achieving the others.

I am aware that I am an infinitesimal speck in the big picture of the universe and my goals do not rate on the universal scale of importance.

Dr Stein rates people's awareness of their insignificance on the universal scale as necessary humility which he says is a sign of being grown up.

Other signs of maturity he mentions are having balance in your life. To be grown up you need to have balance between your heart and your head. You need to have balance between work and having fun. You need to have balance between action and relaxation.

The parts of Dr Stein's essay I found most meaningful include some qualities for which I am striving e.g. To be confident and self-assertive, to take risks and do things which seem too hard, to be able to love and be intimate with another person, liking yourself and appreciating what is good about yourself, accepting your limitations and not denigrating yourself constitute a work in progress for me.

I am nearing the end of my inner journey and I am very grateful to my former lecturer as if it were not for his feedback on my assignment I would not have given attention to the inner Helen or written about my search for the truth.

He also impacted on me when he wrote in his feedback that throughout my assignment he sensed underlying powerful feelings at which I had only hinted.

He said I had rightly given prominence to my achievements however there were also hints at my being embarrassed and humiliated at times and there was a sense that I had also failed.

He pointed out that I had made a throwaway comment on my relationship with my husband by saying that the first twenty years were the worst and he wondered what other things I may have said in that assignment had not loyalty to my husband and the family rules prevented me?

I have now said in this book what I did not say in my assignment.

To do so I had to overcome my feelings of loyalty to my husband and the family rules and confront and dispute my religious indoctrination all of which causes me to feel very anxious.

I am anxious about having left my comfort zone and revealed feelings and personal information I habitually have kept to myself.

Most of all I am anxious about revealing to other people flaws and demons which I am unable to see in myself and leaving myself vulnerable to negative criticism.

I fully accept that although it has been immeasurably valuable to me to have looked at the inside Helen it may not be of value to anyone else including members of my family.

I have been writing "Why am I so angry?" in order to be able

(1) To pay attention to the inside Helen and help her grow up.
(2) To connect with my feelings, particularly my anger.
(3) To find out the reasons for my eating disorder and solve my weight problem and let the weight eventually come off and stay off.

I feel I have achieved most of what I had hoped to achieve by writing this book

I have helped the child Helen to grow up.

I have connected with my feelings especially my anger.

I have found out some of the reasons I developed an eating disorder.

I have discovered I am not to blame and have forgiven myself.

I now understand I had no control over my over eating as it was my automatic response to stress from when I was four years old. It was not my fault as I previously believed that I had become an overweight child and an overweight and at one stage obese adult.

I have not been able to put the past behind me and move into the present as I am still angry about many things including some aspects of my relationship with Jim and there still may be some other sources of my anger. of which I am as yet unaware.

AFTERTHOUGHTS

MORE WOMEN HAVE MORE OPPORTUNITIES and freedom of choice as to how they live their lives. One of the biggest changes has been in the area of sexual morality. Sex is now regarded not as sin but as the birthright of women as well as men.

In spite of the church teachings making up your own mind about how you live your life has now become increasing acceptable for both men and women.

A good example is France's first female former Justice Minister Rachida Dati who it was reported in the SMH November 6th 2012 was during a paternity dispute brought against the alleged father said to have been dating up to eight boyfriends at the time she had her child.

The genuine equality of men and women where women are no longer subjected to the rules and ideas which came about because of the belief in the literal truth of Genesis 2 is obvious and becoming increasingly evident in the developed countries of the world.

This change has happened in the Greek Australian community in Sydney as well.

When I was a teenager most Greek Australian girls were not allowed to openly socialise with boys, work outside the home, have any tertiary education or go to university.

This is no longer the case.

On P.10 of the Weekend Edition of the Sydney Morning Herald 6-8 October 2012 is an article by Lisa Davies who writes that Women

Lawyers had established a record in the number of them being appointed as Senior Counsel.

She says that though diamonds might be a girl's best friend for a record number of Sydney's women barristers silk may have become a satisfying alternative.

Of the twenty six barristers being elevated to the senior ranks of the bar twelve of them are women this year.

One of the women is a Greek Australian who is a Public Defender who was admitted to the NSW Bar in 1989 and who has spent three years with the International Criminal Tribunal.

Many men are involved with their children today as is obvious from visiting a shopping centre particularly on the weekends. It is now not unusual to see a man carrying a baby or pushing a pram or a stroller or looking after two or three young children.

Some men through choice or necessity are the prime carers of the children and look after them and the home while the wife goes to work if she is able to earn more money than he.

Education is the path to progress. There are now more women than men enrolled in many of the University Faculties and more women that are academics or leaders in their field.

There is no longer a clear division between women's work and men's work.

There are now women who are bus drivers, pilots, engineers, Members of Parliament, soldiers, sailors and Marriage celebrants and professors, judges and brain surgeons and there are men who are nurses, primary school teachers, house and office cleaners and prime carers of children.

Professions and occupations are now open to any person who has the aptitude and ability, desire and commitment to pursue them and nobody is now excluded because of their gender.

Much has changed. In my opinion the relationship between women and men can not progress so there is no sexism or misogyny until all men treat all women as equal human beings.

In my opinion this cannot happen until Genesis 2 is no longer taught to children as the only creation story and is replaced by Genesis 1.

Some of my anger has been replaced by compassion however I will remain angry until:

(1) All the Christian churches acknowledge the separate existence of Genesis 1 as a more evolved version of the creation and have adapted what they believe and what they teach accordingly.

(2) Nobody prays to a male God as "Our Father" from that time onwards but to "Our Holy Spirit".

(3) Telling children the story of Adam and Eve without telling them about Genesis Ch1 is prohibited by law.

I am including here a copy of an email my editor Ann sent me after I had sent her the first draft of my book. The Email was dated: Monday 2 May 2011 and is as follows:

"Hi Helen,

Have finally got around to reading your book. Knowing very little about Greek Culture, I found the family history interesting and rather confrontational.

My English background was very different but it also had its difficult moments.

I suppose we're all products of our upbringing to various degrees.

Regarding the "Creation Story" not being taught as absolute truth in schools—I am totally with you on that. I was lucky enough to be sent to a non-denominational school where we mixed with all religions and races and religion was not a big deal. I was horrified to hear your experiences. I am amazed that Australia has so many schools run by different religions.

At home, in my day, the only church affiliated schools were the RC convents, therefore I suppose the rest of us could be considered pagans or infidels and I am quite happy to be thought of as running around in woad and rabbit skins and dancing around Stonehenge on the Summer Solstice.

I thought that your argument against the creation story was well founded and that it would be interesting to start a crusade on the subject.

It is time the pompous religios had a run for their money.

I must admit though that I do like the traditional pomp and circumstance of royal weddings but I thought that the recent royal wedding spawned the worst collection of hats seen in a long time."

When I first went to the Bar I read with a barrister who did Family Law.

He expected me to leave the Bar when I was expecting our seventh child and when I came back three years later I chose to read with a barrister who did Criminal Law.

I am very glad I did because Barry was kind and supportive and very understanding.

I appeared as his junior in criminal matters and because he said "Helen can do that" when one of the accused in a forthcoming trial of six people for murder was unrepresented at that time I was given the brief to defend her. It was the first time I appeared in the Supreme Court as Defence Counsel and my client was the only one of the six accused who was found "Not Guilty."

I later spent two weeks in the Newcastle Supreme Court defending a young woman accused of rape as she had asked a man to rape the girl she thought was responsible for the fact that she herself had been raped. She was found "Guilty" and had to go to gaol however she was pleased with this result.

About a year later when I got off the train in Newcastle where our second daughter was living at that time, I heard someone say "that's my barrister over there" so I stopped and she told me she had been released from prison after six months and they had been good to her while she was in gaol.

This case convinced me I could not work regularly as a barrister.

I was so focused on the case I did not even think of my family for the whole two weeks I spent in Newcastle which is an almost three hour train ride from Sydney.

I only worked when the Registrar of the Bar Association offered me a Crown Assignment and I was relieved I was not offered any more briefs that required me to go so far away.

Crown Assignments were legally assisted criminal cases offered to members of the private Bar and because of this system I was able to appear for people accused of such crimes as Murder, Armed Robbery, Rape, Assault and Negligent Driving.

Some of my clients were found "Guilty" and some "Not guilty" and the "not guilty" verdicts helped me feel the eight years of study had been worthwhile.

When these cases were later only given to Public Defenders I no longer was given any briefs.

I felt I was not destined to be a practising barrister as I had no family connections except two solicitor cousins who could not brief me as they did not do criminal law work.

I knew I could never be a solicitor myself. The six months I spent at the College of Law were the longest six months of my life and I could well understand why some solicitors escaped the stress by absconding with the trust funds and am amazed that not more of them do so.

In every case I found it very stressful when I was in a trial and felt I "died a thousand deaths" every time we were waiting for the Jury to come back with its verdict.

I felt happiest and most fulfilled whenever I was expecting a baby and/or passing exams. I felt this is what I was born to do

I did not feel I was destined to be a stay-at-home mother though I admired women who felt fulfilled doing so

I did not have the ability or dedication to be a teacher or an academic though I liked studying.

When I had left the Bar and the children had grown up I enrolled in the Counselling and Therapy course which I felt was the best and most beneficial course I had ever done. However the most important life-changing fulfilling achievement of my life was my becoming a mother.

I am very grateful after a false start we were able to have seven healthy children.

My first labour lasted thirty six hours. I did not know whether I was in labour or was just suffering from a form of colic. I delayed going to the hospital until almost the last minute. I did not see the birth as a sister put a mask on my face so the baby would not be born until my doctor had arrived. All my other labours except the last one were so quick and easy one of the sisters said to me "I wish they were all like you".

My last labour was a breach birth and three weeks early because I had tripped in the kitchen and had fallen flat on my tummy.

I was very grateful for the first time in my life for the extra padding of fat on my tummy when I heard one woman's baby had died after she had had a similar fall.

I knew it was time for me to stop having any more children.

Were it not for the thoughtfulness and generosity of my father I would not have been able to do anything other than get married and stay home.

He not only provided a small income for me, he set up a trust for his grandchildren and because of this trust we were able to send all our children to private schools.

We thought this was the right thing to do and now we are not so sure.

I am sad we spent all that money when according to an article in the press, some private schools employed as teachers people who were not qualified as teachers.

I agree with our former Prime Minister Julia Gillard that every child in Australia deserves the best possible education

I am sad I only had the best possible education when I was an adult and by that time I feel it was too late for me to be able to make the best use of it

I am sad because in a world where success is measured by how much money a person earns, I am a complete failure.

To me it is enough that I was the first Greek Australian woman to be have been admitted to the Bar of New South Wales when there were only three other women practising at that time.

Because of the talent and hard work of Juliette Brodsky who is a Journalist and Media Consultant, I am in the Oral History of the Pioneering Women at the NSW Bar 1921 to1975.

Father was not a lawyer though he would have been had he had the opportunity to study. As a young man he attended the Law Courts as an Interpreter and greatly admired the barristers he told me.

Because he was such a successful business man who started the popular trend of Milk Bars in Australia I was able to enable him to vicariously fulfil his own desire to be a barrister. I am glad a photo of the Black and White Milk Bar, Martin Place is in the history of the first twenty five women at the Bar of NSW. This history was due to the initiative of the NSW Bar Association Women Barristers Forum which helps and supports and promotes equality of opportunity for the now over 475 women, one of whom was tragically killed during the Siege in Martin Place on the 16th December 2014.

I am frustrated I was not able to commit myself to being a full time barrister and will never know whether I would have been a successful barrister or not however I do not regret any of the choices I have made.

ON THE WAY TO COURT TO BE ADMITTED
TO THE BAR OF N.S.W.

WITH MY FATHER AND JIM AFTER MY
ADMISSION TO THE BAR OF N.S.W.

I left the Bar with the intention of practising as a Mediator.

I had done a number of mediation courses and workshops however none of them included a practicum so I did not feel equipped to even try going into practice.

When I had completed the two year Jansen Newman Counselling course which did include a practicum I felt I had found my true vocation.

I asked for and was given the practical training at the Burwood Probation and Parole office.

After I had graduated I applied for and was given work as a counsellor there one day a week for fourteen months under contract to the Department of Corrective Services.

After that I was accepted as a volunteer Face to Face Counsellor at Lifeline on a twelve month contract when they were based in Surry Hills.

I was returning home from Lifeline on the 30th March 2009 and when I got to Bondi Junction I found our street had been cordoned off by the police. I could not cross the street. There were people bunched along the footpath looking up at our apartments outside of which there was a Fire truck and a ladder to the top of the building.

Police cars and other fire engines were blocking the street and police, reporters and camera men mingled with the crowds and someone said there had been a huge explosion on the top floor and all the residents had been evacuated

As soon as the crowds had dispersed and things had seemingly returned to normal except in me I immediately took myself to the shopping centre and bought a prepaid mobile phone so I could contact Jim and other family members none of whom knew where I was.

Over three hundred people were left homeless and had to find alternative accommodation.

We were not let back into our apartments until the 23rd November that year.

All our dead plants on the balcony were taken away by a team of men who had come to check for damage and to clean our apartment.

I replaced all the plants and brought big plants and big bags of soil and enjoyed getting everything back to order which took a lot of heavy lifting and a lot more energy than usual.

I went through considerable pain until I saw a doctor who ordered a blood test and told me I had polymyalgia. I had to take medication to get back to normal which took a few months.

When I was at the Bar the least stressful and happiest time for me was when I sold my chambers, crossed Phillip Street and leased a small area on the fourth floor of the building which had replaced the old Law School. My bank gave me an overdraft and after I had designed and arranged for the construction of a small set of chambers for six barristers I formed a company eventually called University Chambers Fourth Floor.

I enjoyed being in charge of this project for three years. I was not offered any briefs during this time and I did not make any money however it was a rewarding and fulfilling experience.

More barristers established chambers on three other floors of the building.

Although I felt pleased I had initiated the use of the old Law school for use as chambers not everyone at the Bar thought it was as appropriate as I did.

GRADUATION AS MASTER OF ARTS
AT THE UNIVERSITY OF NSW

for which I had passed six subjects in Women's Studies gaining
four Distinctions and two Credits unlike during the Law course
in which I was a straight P student where P stood for either a
pass or a post of which I had been given seven in eight years.

WITH OUR FOUR YOUNGER CHILDREN.

PHOTO TAKEN BY JACQUI ON THE
OCCASION OF MICHAEL'S BIRTHDAY

WHEN ALL THE CHILDREN WERE STILL LIVING AT HOME.

Photo taken by Jacqui on our Sixtieth Wedding Anniversary.
Jennifer who lives in San Diego joined us on Skype.

At this stage of my life I wonder when and how I am going to die but I am not afraid of the act of dying as I almost died at the time of my miscarriage and I almost died again about seven years ago.

I had visited Jim who was recovering from heart surgery in St Vincent's Hospital and as it was my birthday I decided to take myself to lunch.

While I was waiting, a man said to me "Have you tried the Calamari rings? They are the best I have ever tasted."

Usually whenever I have inadvertently eaten food containing monosodium glutamate (MSG) it takes my having to stay in bed for three days with nausea and dizziness before I recover.

This time I felt so ill after I had eaten the calamari I had to phone for an ambulance.

I lapsed in and out of consciousness all night I was told when I found myself in Intensive Care the next morning.

One of the sisters said had I not rung the ambulance when I did, I would have collapsed at home and would not have survived.

I am angry the government has not banned the use of Monosodium Glutamate MSG.

At least one young person who had asthma has died because of it and many people who are intolerant of it should they react like I do would have wished they would die when they were suffering from the effects of it.

I do not understand why enhancing the flavour of food for perhaps the majority of people is more important than protecting possibly the life and well being of a minority of people. Surely needless and untimely deaths and/or suffering need to be prevented?

Today is the eighth of March, International Women's Day 2013 and I have finished writing my book!

I feel it may be enough just to leave copies for my family and trust if or when they read it they will not feel my writing it has been a complete waste of time and has been worthwhile.

Whether or not anyone else reads what I have written I feel I have achieved something worthwhile by writing it.

It has been very therapeutic for me.

I feel I will now be able to satisfy my curiosity as to what my natural weight was meant to be had my eating disorder not taken over my life from when I was four years old.

I wanted to finish the book before Jim had his operation for a hip replacement and I needed to put everything on hold until he had completely recovered.

He has had his operation and is now well on the road to recovery and I am checking and rechecking what I have written while he has been sleeping during the day.

He is not sleeping much during the night as he has to sleep on his back because he is not allowed to sleep on his side for six weeks. I am using this opportunity not only to recheck what I have already written but to look further inside myself to write about what comes into my mind.

The first thing to come to mind is when my father died on the 14th December 1969.

My mother rang us in the middle of the night and said in a very agitated tone of voice "Come quickly! Your father is having an attack and needs help."

Jim rang our friend who is a doctor and lived in our area and went off to pick him up and take him to my parent's home. I had to stay with the children and I sat by the telephone unable to move until Jim rang me to say my father had died of a heart attack and there was nothing more they could have done and he was bringing my mother home with him.

I still sat by the phone until they arrived.

My mother stayed with us for a year then my sister and her husband who also lived in the same suburb in a single story home decided they could add a granny flat upstairs for our mother who paid for the addition.

My sister had young children too and my mother seemed very happy there as she felt at home and felt independent. She liked catching the bus to Bondi Junction nearly every day and we would often have lunch or coffee with her and our uncle Ernest her brother in law whose wife had also died.

Everything was OK until my mother fell and broke her leg. When she came out of hospital she could no longer go up the stairs to her flat and lived downstairs in their spare room.

My sister was given an ultimatum by her husband "Either she goes or I go" so my mother came back to live with us for almost the last five years of her life.

There was a Mediation Conference and Course in Vancouver I very much wanted to attend and my sister said she could not take our mother to her place so I didn't know what I could do.

The sister of a friend of ours was a nurse and was working at the Castellorizian Nursing Home which she said was excellent so we made enquiries and for the last eight months of her life my mother lived there.

The matron told us she was very helpful to her as she was able to translate into English for the women who only speak Greek. When we asked our mother if she wanted to come home again she said she did not want to come home as she was very happy where she was.

I am angry about the whole situation and I feel guilty about my mother living in a home even for a relatively short time of eight months of her life.

As soon as we returned from Vancouver later we took her out for coffee and a walk at a shopping centre. I felt guilty as she seemed to have deteriorated while we were away and she looked older and unwell.

Next morning matron phoned that mother had collapsed and they had called an ambulance.

We met mum at the hospital and she spoke to both of us.

She looked very sick and her face was yellow.

We were told to wait outside in the waiting room while they did some tests.

During this time the doctor came out to tell us she had died while she was talking to him and did we want him to try to resuscitate her?

I replied that she was ninety three years old and I did not think it was necessary to do so.

I was not sure I had made the right decision until we were asked did we wish to see her.

I am glad we did as her colour had returned to normal and she looked relaxed, happy, young and beautiful again.

My sister wanted to have the funeral as soon as possible which was on a Tuesday.

I changed it to Wednesday as my mother never started anything on a Tuesday. This was a Greek tradition as an unsuccessful war against the Turks had been started on a Tuesday.

My sister rang the Funeral parlour and changed it back to Tuesday as she had arranged for all her friends to help her and it was more convenient for her and for them on the Tuesday.

I am angry about that and expressed my anger at the time by sitting at the back of the church and not going to the cemetery.

Perhaps it would have been better had I been able to express myself assertively however I do not see the point of doing so when I feel the situation can not be changed.

This is certainly the case in my relationship with Jim.

He can not change what his primary interests are. I am not able to change the fact that I do not share them. Even though I am being unreasonable I can not stop my feeling angry.

I am angry every time I see him studying the Sport's pages. The first time I remember being aware of his doing so was when we were living in New Zealand when we were first married.

I am angry having to listen to football talk at any time particularly when we are at lunch with his sister Connie.

I am angry when I think of every time I wanted to go to a concert, the theatre or a movie and I had to go on my own or stay home because he had to watch the football.

I am angry every time I hear music to which I would love to dance and I move around the room on my own as he continues to read the paper.

I am angry when I read about the benefits of ballroom dancing and I remember how he refused to even attempt to learn to dance.

I am angry when he gets up early to watch the golf and seems so enthralled with it and with every football game he watches particularly the All Blacks playing Rugby.

I am angry his priorities never change even when we are on holiday.

Watching the sport has been and still is more important to him than I am it seems to me.

The inside Helen is still angry.

The inside Helen is affectionate, gregarious, attractive, fun loving, adventurous, positive and enthusiastic and is angry she is not able to be her true self and is not really living but is existing in an isolated emotional desert.

In an article in the SMH Good Weekend 24th August 2013 called "No Sex, Please", Benjamin Law refers to a British Study of 18,000 people about their sexual practices which found that 1 percent of them had never been sexually attracted to anyone.

The cause of asexuality is unknown however possible causes were self-reported to be sexual abuse, sexual confusion or not having found the right partner.

Could another possible cause be belief in the literal truth of the Adam and Eve version of the creation?

I do not feel I am asexual however I do not feel sexually normal and I wonder if this is because of the indoctrination at the school I attended or because of any of the stated possible causes of asexuality mentioned in the article?

My father had told me nobody would marry me unless I lost weight. My subconscious would not accept that and I proved my father wrong by being the only overweight girl in our community at that time to be married, even before the slim attractive girls.

At all the weddings I had ever attended it seemed to be the custom when talking about the bride to always comment on how beautiful she is or looks.

At my wedding the Greek Orthodox Archbishop (who was a friend of my father) when referring to me said in Greek "In Helen we see an example of a kind, thoughtful, compassionate, talented, very intelligent good human being." and I was very happy about his saying that even though I knew why he had said it.

Having had the Family Movie Videos converted into DVD's recently I have been looking at some of them including the one of our wedding in which I looked fatter or slimmer according to the angle at which the movie was taken for which I was very grateful.

I was very grateful I looked fatter or slimmer according to how the photos were taken too as is illustrated in the photos below.

Throughout my life for as long as I can remember I have been going up and down in weight not because that is what I wanted to do but because of my reaction to the situation in which I found myself in at the time.

I felt abnormal and unacceptable because of my body and my inability to control how it looked.

I wanted to be loved and I felt this would not happen until I lost weight and I could not lose weight by trying to do so as it was not my conscious desire which determined my weight.

By looking at the family movies I could see the first time I looked slim was after I had left Jim and Wellington and had been back in Sydney for at least three to four months.

The first time I looked really overweight was when I had had my second child and I was studying for Post exams which I had been given because my doctor had written to the Dean of the Law school saying our baby was due in the middle of the exams in November.

I was also up in weight in the movie of me with our four older children the last two of whom had been born in the same year—one in January and one in December—and I was studying for exams.

I was medium weight for my Graduations.

I was most slim in the movie of our overseas trip with Connie after I had been working outside the home for over a year.

When I was up in weight I judged myself as an undisciplined glutton and I felt I was being judged as such by other people too when the truth was I had no control over my overeating and felt I neither deserved blame for when I was up or praise for when I was down.

The only person who did not comment on my weight through the years was Jim who told me he did not notice the changes. He has never said "I love you" to me and I have never said "I love you" to him however we have formed a strong bond over the years and I feel his good sense of humour and his attractive smile helped. Having a good father for my children was my top priority and he has exceeded my expectations in that regard.

I did not know why I was not stable in weight like other people and now I know it was because I had an undiagnosed Binge Eating Disorder since childhood. I know it is part of who I am and I am more accepting of it, now that I know more about it.

Even though I am coming to the end of writing my book I am not coming to the end of my search for the truth. Although looking at the inside Helen has been of great benefit to me it has not eliminated my eating problem as yet and I am still looking for answers.

8

CONCLUSION

I FEEL I HAVE BENEFITED very much from following my former lecturer's suggestions to pay attention to the inside Helen to connect with my feelings and help the inside Helen who may still be a little girl to grow up.

Since I officially finished the book on the 8th March 2013 there have been at least two major and important developments which I am now able to include.

The Royal Commission which our then Prime Minister announced in November last year commenced this year on the 3rd April 2013.

Justice Peter McClennan opened the Commission in the Melbourne County Court explaining the way the commission would proceed.

The plan is to have five months of private hearings before one or two of the commissioners so the victims are able to tell their story in an non-adversarial environment and this would inform the six commissioners of the extent of the problem on which they are expected to ultimately make a finding at the end of three years.

The expected number of people who will give evidence before the commission is five thousand. To date, there had been twelve hundred phone calls made on the royal commission hot line.

I personally have no recollection of ever having been sexually abused as a child however I do not remember what happened to me when we were living in Athens from the time I was eighteen months old until I was almost three years old.

During my inner journey I have become aware that some experts believe that eating disorders are the result of repressed childhood sexual abuse.

Some of the attitudes and behaviours such a person displays are ones which I recognise in myself such as dislike and fear of one's body, dislike of being touched by anyone, low self esteem, preferring one's own company to that of other people, hiding oneself behind layers of fat and perhaps over-eating because of the need for space—not food. During my search for the truth I have become aware that these attitudes and behaviours may also be the result of a person having been born an introvert

My being an introvert way of knowing the real reason for my eating disorder no matter how many theories exist and how many factors I feel contributed.

My being an introvert explains to me why when Jim and I went away to discover our roots before we settled in Sydney and we were in each others company twenty four hours a day for four months I was unable to control my over-eating and my weight peaked at ninety five kilos.

It was a very unhappy time for me and I trust I am more assertive and self aware now and not likely to be in the position I was in then ever again.

I regret I did not get the benefit from the trip I would like to have had.

Perhaps this is because I felt so emotionally insecure with Jim I needed to comfort myself with food and was unable to feel happy with him no matter where we were.

The second very important thing which happened is that the New Zealand National Party with the support of the Labour Opposition passed a law on the 17th April 2013 by seventy seven votes to forty four legalising marriage between same sex couples.

The next day on the 14th April 2013 the front page of the Sydney Morning Herald featured the news that the Liberal Premier of NSW has changed his mind and now supports same sex marriage and is of the opinion the Federal Opposition should allow its members to have a conscience vote. Their leader Tony Abbott said he may consider doing that after the election in September. Since then the former Prime Minister Kevin Rudd has changed his mind and now agrees with the rest of his family that same sex marriage needs to be legalised.

New Zealand has again led the way and is the first country in the Pacific Region to legalise same sex marriage. Jim who was born and grew up in Wellington New Zealand often reminds me that New Zealand gave women the right to vote in 1893 before any other country.

In view of the public support for same sex marriage it seems certain it will not be too long before Australia joins the thirteen countries and nine states in America which have legalised it. In the meantime it would be a step in the right direction should now Australia recognise the same sex marriages which took or take place in any country in which they are legal.

I agree with Ecclesiastes 3 which states that for everything there is a season and a time for everything in the universe. The time has come for same sex marriage to be accepted.

The time has also come for the truth about the consequences of some of the teachings of the Catholic church to be fully exposed and remedied.

An article on page 12 of the Sun Herald by Matt Wade on the 21st April 2013 states that research has shown that the male breadwinner role model is stronger in Australia than in many other comparable countries including the USA where the dual earner model has been accepted and is becoming the norm.

He says in Australia 85% of men whose youngest child was under the age of five worked full time while the percentage of women in that situation was only about 19 % This article seems to suggest if there were more available and affordable child care then mothers of young children could become full time members of the workforce too and so close the gap between the earning capacity of the men and women.

I feel this would neither be in the best interests of young children who need to attach to a parent rather than other people or to their mothers who need time to bond with their babies and most of whom would prefer not to have to leave their young children.

In my opinion true equality between women and men could only become universal through education of girls and boys which in theory and practice equips them to fulfil the role of looking after the home and children and have a fulfilling profession and successful career or job in the work place. The solution to the problem of women not being able to earn as much as men is not for the women to work full time but for both men and women to work part time inside the home and part time outside the home by making part-time work the norm.

Women would not feel guilty about leaving their young children if they were in the care of their partner. When both partners are responsible for caring for the children and the home and both partners are responsible for earning the money then there is true equality for both men and women as is their birthright according to Genesis 1 whose time has also now come.

Women have evolved or were made by a male and female God at the same time so God is within women as well as men. I feel it is the role of education to discover the way to develop our individual talents and abilities and help us develop our full potential according to who we were born to be. We were not all born evil because Adam and Eve disobeyed God. The story of Adam and Eve is not literally true.

Women are not even in theory the chattels of men in our modern world and their equal status which is increasingly being demonstrated needs to be acknowledged and respected.

When there is real equality women will not need to delay having a family until they are older.

I know from personal experience and our children will attest to the the fact that I was a much better mother to the first four children who were born in five years than I was to the last three children born several years later when I did not have as much energy. It was much harder for me and it was harder for the younger children who do not have the happy memories of their childhood that the older ones have.

Our youngest child told me angrily that if I did not have the time to be a real mother to my children I should not have had them. I was so driven to have more children it did not occur to me to stop and think about it.

I am glad I followed my feelings and my intuition.

In spite of all the problems and hassles I am glad I was able to do what I wanted to do.

I was passionate about having children and going to University and I am grateful I was eventually able to do both and have a fulfilling life even if I am angry about some parts of it.

Soon after my first graduation I was on the bus when Maureen who had been my best friend in High school and was married with five children and whom I had not seen since the twenty five year school reunion sat next to me to tell me she was on her way to enrol at the University of NSW because she told herself if Helen can do it so can I.

Next time I saw her by chance on the 400 bus she had just graduated as a Bachelor of Arts!

I am very grateful I could achieve what I wanted to achieve by following my intuition which to me is the divine spark which is in all of us and more important I feel than following the example of others and being part of the crowd.

I have often found if I follow my intuition or my hunches God or the Universe seems to help me to succeed and if I have inadvertently made the wrong decision obstacles block my way.

If at least one person reads this book and questions the validity of the story of Adam and Eve and substitutes the principle of Genesis 1 for that of Genesis 2 perhaps more people will question the teachings of the Catholic church especially in view of the revelations about child abuse and will demand it changes its teachings so all women are treated as equal human beings with the same right to achieve their potential as the men even in the Priesthood.

How could this come about while the story of Adam and Eve is still being told to any children and is part of our culture and Genesis Ch1 is not?

Why was the first woman Prime Minister of Australia so unpopular?

Was it because of the way she became Prime Minister in the first place or could it have been because she was a woman in a population in which perhaps most people had been indoctrinated with the Genesis 2 version of the creation and had never heard of Genesis Ch1?

If this was so, how could this indoctrination have led to anything other than the Misogyny to which she was so often subjected?

Kevin Rudd was reinstated as Prime Minister by fifty seven to forty five votes on June twenty sixth 2013 and as Julia Gillard herself said the fact she had been Prime Minister will make it easier for the next woman Prime Minister of Australia and for the woman after her as well.

I am angry at the way Julia Gillard was treated as Prime Minister. I feel that when Genesis 1 supplants Genesis 2 in the hearts and minds of most Australians the next woman Prime Minister will be more welcome and more enthusiastically accepted and respected than our first woman PM in spite of her valuable and remarkable achievements which have been acknowledged by many people especially Kevin Rudd.

Why was there a campaign against Julia Gillard which not only showed disrespect for her personally but for the office of Prime Minister?

I find it hard to imagine this would have happened in a society which acknowledged the inherent equality of men and women as is it in Genesis 1.

I feel that only a man brought up to believe the story of Adam and Eve is literally true would have addressed a crowd, standing in front of banners with the words "Ditch the Witch" and "Bob Brown's Bitch" on them about Julia Gillard.

I feel that Julia Gillard's greatest achievement was the establishment of the Royal Commission on the Sexual abuse of Children.

Perhaps what is needed is a Royal Commission into how many children in Australia are being told the Genesis 2 Adam and Eve story of the creation is the literal truth and are not being told of the existence of Genesis 1 and how many adults still believe in the truth of the story of Adam and Eve and have never heard of Genesis 1.

As from the 7th September 2013 there has been a change of Government in Australia and the new Prime Minister is the former Leader of the Opposition Tony Abbott who is a devout Catholic and at one time was studying to become a Priest. I believe he will neither support legislation to stop children being indoctrinated with belief in Genesis 2 as the truth nor will he consider that men and women were created equal by a God who is both male and female.

Because of who he is, I doubt he would value the scientific evidence about climate change or homosexuality—the right to abortion—same sex marriage—or euthanasia—as the majority of Australians, according to the polls, now do.

I am no longer only angry about the past. I am now angry about the present and what may or may not happen in the future.

The good news is that if the majority of the Australian People is not happy with this Newly Elected Government we only have to wait three years under the present rules before we are able to change it.

9

UPDATE

The book Why Am I So Angry? My Search for The Truth was first published in October 2013 and it was republished in March 2014 with an additional paragraph.

I had distributed copies of the book to all the members of our family and to some relatives and friends. The reason I wrote the extra paragraph was because when I gave a copy of the book to our second daughter, she told me that the Catholic Church had changed- it no longer told children the story of Adam and Eve was literally true. I wanted to tell her and everyone else, that by not telling children about the existence of Genesis 1, the Catholic Church was nevertheless still discriminating against women.

When I gave our eldest daughter a copy of my book she said "Why are you giving me this? I do not have an anger problem". I had not realised the title of the book could be interpreted in the way that she had. In any case, as I am no longer so angry now, I have left some of my anger out of this edition.

My sister told me she had no recollection of having been told the story of Adam and Eve at school and if she had been, she said, she had "brushed it off." She said she felt I had been "damaged" by what I had been told and concluded the nuns had really "Got" to me whereas they had "Not gotten" to her. I was not surprised she had lent my book to her children however I was surprised they had read it and liked it, whereas most of our children just ignored it

One of Jim's sisters said to him "The trouble with Helen is that she takes things too seriously." His other sister told me it was very hard for her to accept that Jim and I did not love each other and she was not sure that an "everlasting bond between us "which I told her we have, makes up for the lack of love. Perhaps it depends on what each person believes the word "Love" means?

One friend rang to tell me she had read my book on Kindle and she had felt very upset because it was personal and private and in her opinion it would have been better had I not had it published. Another friend told me I should go down on my knees and thank God for my childhood, which was so much better than his had been. Several people, including Jim himself, told me that I had been "hard on Jim." One cousin, who had gone to a Catholic school, told me how much she empathised with what I had written about my school.

Another cousin told me how much she could empathise with what I had written about our Youth Club. My cousin who had been the Director of a Kindergarten rang to tell me "I have been thinking about your book and I have come to the conclusion that you were a Gifted Child at a time when such children were not recognised and that is why you were so unhappy at school." I told her if she were to be right, which I doubted, this would have made the situation worse, not better in my opinion. My cousin in Queensland's letter about my book was published in the local paper and the book is in the library for which I am indebted to her.

On the whole I was left with the feeling that I was in a "blame the victim" situation similar to where there has been child abuse. I felt I was being told either directly or indirectly that all my suffering was my own fault. I was the one who was in the wrong because of who I am and for reacting the way I did.

Even my ex-lecturer, in his letter thanking me for sending him a copy of the book, said he found himself wondering how many children would have taken the story of Adam and Eve as literally as I did—and

I guess the answer to that question could be—"Perhaps most, if not all the little introverted girls and boys who were told that story was the truth."

Then he went on to say but he still hears adult clients, very often, talking about fear of Hell that was instilled into them by early teaching (usually Catholic, but often Protestant also) and how it sits uneasily at the back of their minds. He said they don't usually talk about how their attitudes to gender might have been similarly affected, but he does not doubt the possibility that they may have been. I feel very strongly that they have been and in my case I feel not only my attitude to gender but my attitude to sexuality has been affected as well.

He said he agrees that Genesis 1 is less sexist than Genesis 2. He is not sure he agrees with all my interpretations of Genesis 1, but he certainly agrees that it has suited the Christian Church to teach Genesis 2 as one of its central myths to support and justify the dominance of men over women and of human beings over all other forms of life.

The only person, other than our eldest son and his partner, who seemed to agree with what I believe about the negative influence of the story of Adam and Eve, was a cousin of Jim's by marriage. In her email to me after she had read the book she said: "As for your theories on Genesis 1 and 2 not having been directly/consciously influenced by the teachings about Eve's innate inferiority, I cannot really give an opinion. Except that I have often marvelled that women past and even present can get out of bed in the mornings, such was/is the weight of oppression. So subliminally, if not explicitly, I guess we have all been influenced by the teachings of Genesis 2." This is exactly what I wanted to make people aware of, so I am happy I succeeded with at least one person.

I am also grateful to her for offering to edit the book and spending so much of her time and effort in doing so which I very much appreciate. She has not only been very helpful. It is because of her help that I was motivated to revise the book.

It might be simplistic to blame the teaching of the Adam and Eve myth as the truth to children, as the reason for Domestic Violence, Sexual Harassment, Sexual Assaults of Women and Children, the

Sexual Dysfunction in some men and women, the Belief in the Innate Superiority of men, Misogyny, the Subordination of Women and their previous exclusion from the universities, the priesthood and other occupations. However I find it very hard to imagine how it could NOT have had a wide-ranging conscious or subconscious negative effect on men /women relations and on how women have been and some of them still are, regarded and treated in our culture.

My ex lecturer had started his letter by telling me he was glad I took his suggestions on my Differentiation of Self assignment so seriously, as I had obviously gained quite a lot of insight from the process. He said he was sorry that the process was only partially successful in assisting me to change my behaviour in this area of my life which causes me so much distress. In reply I told him the reason the process had only been partly successful was because I felt there was more that I had to do in order to complete the process. That is why I had registered to attend a two day seminar called "Overcoming Trauma-Related Shame and Self-Loathing" to be held later in the year on 10-11 November 2014.

I felt attending this seminar would help me, as on the back of the brochure it stated this intensive 2-day training provides the opportunity for detailed exploration of effective interventions with inter alia, Eating and Somatoform Disorders; Substance Abuse and Addiction; and Individuals struggling with Interpersonal Relationships and Fulfilment - all of which are of special interest to me. I was very much looking forward to it.

In the meantime I took the advice of my God- daughter, who having read my book suggested that I read: The Closing of the Western Mind. The Rise of Faith and the Fall of Reason. Charles Freeman. Vintage Books 2005 A Division of Random House, Inc. New York.

This book is not my kind of book and it was hard for me to even skim through it until I reached Chapter 16 and then I became and will forever be very grateful to Anita for telling me about this book. Until I read Chapter 16—The Ascetic Odyssey—I had been unable to understand why it is that the existence of Genesis 1 seems to have been completely ignored by the Christian Churches and I now know and understand how and why this has come about.

The author explains how from the Fourth Century AD when the Emperor Constantine converted to Christianity and declared it the official religion of the Roman Empire, the Christian leaders needed to firmly establish the orthodoxy of the Church and solidify their position within the state.

This drove them to stifle any debate or dissent and to cover up and ignore any doctrinal contradictions. The Church was becoming very wealthy, as was demonstrated by their program of building some of the most costly edifices in Europe and this was in contrast to the Ascetics, who renounced wealth and subjugated their physical desires, in order to become spiritually transformed and closer to God. Like the martyrs before them, they believed they had to suffer as a mark of their faith.

One of the results of the rise of the cult of the Virgin Mary and the elevation of virginity at that time, the author says, was that while Mary was very highly regarded, women as a whole, were regarded as having been cursed by God as Eve had been, for breaking God's Commandment.

Women were considered to be either Virgins or Whores and this approach to sexuality still influences the Christian tradition, he says. One committed Christian who refused to endorse this view was a Monk from Rome whose name was Jovinian.

This man was a down to earth, realistic person whose views were very popular at that time. He had been an ascetic who had later renounced asceticism as being spiritually meaningless. He saw no reason why people should not enjoy eating and drinking freely as long as they offered thanks to God for their good fortune and he asked the question " Why would married women be regarded less highly than virgins in the eyes of God?"

He ridiculed the idea that Mary had remained physically a virgin after she had given birth. He also pointed out that right at the beginning of the Bible, there is Genesis 1- in which there is no sexual restriction or rejection of sexuality. Male and female were ordered by God, to be fruitful and multiply.

One of the powerful Christian leaders was outraged by the ideas of Jovinian and viciously attacked both him and his book. Charles Freeman says (p244) Jovinian was declared a heretic, ordered to be flogged with leaden whips and forced to leave Rome for Milan.

There he was also attacked by a fervent defender of the superiority of Virginity over Marriage, so Jovinian's counter attack had failed, and Sex and Sin remained forever linked in the Christian tradition. I was shocked when I read about how Jovinian had been treated.

I wonder had I been baptised a Catholic, would I be excommunicated and considered to be a heretic for bringing attention to the existence of Genesis 1, thus challenging the legitimacy and validity of Genesis 2 as the foundation on which the Catholic Church has been built?

Even though I had not been baptised a Catholic and had not even attended the religious doctrine classes, I feel very guilty criticising the Catholic Church as I do. Going to a Catholic school has left indelible marks on me. Some of their beliefs have influenced me at least on a subconscious level as why else would I have felt when I became engaged, that by doing so I had lost my "specialness" in the eyes of God who would have regarded me more highly had I stayed single and celibate?

I know of one committed Catholic pharmacist who would not sell condoms or any contraceptives because contraception was against his religion. It seems to me that most committed Catholics oppose Abortion, Homosexuality, Same Sex Marriage and Euthanasia on the same basis, without thinking of the pros and cons of each or any one of them. *I had my doubts about Abortion until I attended the trial of Dr Smart who helped women by doing abortions when it was illegal to do so.*

As I listened to the women and why each of them had decided to have an abortion, it seemed to me it was not what they wanted to do but in the circumstances, it was what they had to do, as they felt there was no acceptable alternative.

Surely it is the women whose lives are most affected who need the right to make these decisions, not the men in Church or Parliament?

The Church is protecting the right to life of the unborn child without considering how being an unwanted child affects the future life of that child.

I remember reading about a study which showed that most of the children of women who had been refused an abortion, ended up in the prison system. I do not remember when or where the study was done however I read about it when I was studying Criminology.

As prohibiting abortion can be shown to be detrimental to both mother and child, how would giving women the sole right to decide whether or not to have an abortion not be in the best interest of society?

The Pope as head of the Catholic Church has the authority to make rules only for Catholics I believe, so I was happy to read in The Sydney Morning Herald on the Fourth of November 2014 on P9 News Death with Dignity. Legal drugs used to end life. TERMINALLY ILL CANCER SUFFERER DIES AT HOME, BUCKET LIST DONE"- an article by Jenna Clarke.

This article is about Brittany Maynard, a 29 year old American woman with brain cancer who chose to end her life by using drugs made legal by the State of Oregon's Death with Dignity Act. She had been given six months to live so she, her husband and her parents moved from San Francisco to Oregon. She had done a lot of research into all her available options after the tumour returned two months after surgery. She knew how painful her life would be if prolonged by chemotherapy or radiation treatment. She considered going into a Hospice however realised she could develop morphine resistant pain and suffer if she opted for palliative care. She completed her Bucket List, which included establishing The Brittany Maynard Fund which her family will use to fight for Death with Dignity laws in other states of America. She then, with the support of her family, took the life- ending medication which was her moral and legal right to do, when she felt it was the right time for her to do so.

How could what she did be, in Pope Francis' words "Against God and creation"? Why should other people in the same situation be legally prohibited from doing what she did? The Sydney Morning Herald,

November 17th 2014 under WORLD p13 had a short report at the top of the page under the heading POPE SPEAKS OUT AGAINST EUTHANASIA. This states that Pope Francis in his address to the Association of Italian Catholic Doctors has denounced the right-to-die movement, saying it is a false sense of compassion to consider euthanasia as an act of dignity, when it is a sin against God and creation. He also condemned abortion, in vitro fertilisation and embryonic stem cell research as playing with life which is a sin against the creator, against God the creator, he said.

I do not believe the Pope has the moral right to be the arbiter of what is right or wrong in "the eyes of God". His Church has been covering up the sexual abuse of children in their care for many years. Why was what was right or wrong " in the eyes of God" not considered to be relevant during all the time the abuse of children (and women) by the Priests and Brothers of the Catholic Church was taking place?

I was sad to read on P10 News in the Sydney Morning Herald, January 9 2015 that High school teachers need more guidelines to help them tackle homophobia, the review of a NSW pilot program found, according to the article by Amy McNeilage.

The NSW Government had abandoned the Proud Schools initiative in 12 public schools between 2011 and 2013 which had had a positive influence on their school, two thirds of the students surveyed had said, reducing homophobic language and encouraging greater acceptance of gay, lesbian, transgender and intersex students.

The pilot schools said they wanted stronger leadership from the NSW Education Department, the President of which said it would need a policy backed up with professional consultants employed full time to support teachers on how to deal with homophobia because homophobia is one of the worst causes of teenage suicide.

A recent survey of same- sex attracted and gender diverse young people found homophobic bullying was rife in schools, especially in the physical education lessons where 98% per cent of students had heard casual homophobia. Almost half of these students had thought of self- harm or suicide and about 14 percent had attempted suicide.

Personally, I do not understand how the Federal Government's employment of Chaplains in schools instead of Psychologists and Counsellors, could possibly help teachers deal with homophobia when it seems the teachings of Christian Churches about homosexuality is the basic cause of it.

The two day Seminar on the 10th-11th November 2014 was presented by Dr Janine Fisher who is a Clinical Psychologist and Instructor at the Trauma Center and is Assistant Director of the Sensorimotor Psychotherapy Institute in America. My impression of Dr Fisher was that she was a very well-informed and experienced therapist who was caring, loving and compassionate and able to genuinely help traumatised people who came to her for therapy.

We were shown slides to which she spoke as we read the text in our workbooks and she showed us two videos of Therapy Sessions— one by her and one by another therapist demonstrating Sensorimotor Psychotherapy. The most helpful and important information I gained was from reading her two papers which were included in the material we were given : The Anatomy of Self Hatred: Learning to Love Our Loathed Selves – Published in Psychotherapy networker, July/August 2012 and SELF – HARM AND SUICIDALITY which paper had been presented at The Trauma Center Lecture Series, Boston, Mass

The definition of Sensorimotor Psychotherapy in Wikipedia states that this therapy was developed by Dr Pat Ogden who founded the Sensorimotor Institute in 1981 and has been internationally acclaimed as a comprehensive somatic psychotherapy method for healing the disconnect between body and mind that occurs as a result of trauma or attachment failure. It draws from somatic therapies, neuroscience, attachment theory and cognitive approaches as well as from Hakomi Therapy.

By attending this two day seminar I feel I have found the piece of the puzzle which was previously missing during my search for the truth and which I needed in order to be able to complete the process and get the full benefit from looking within myself.

I learned that my eating problem was more than likely a symptom of an early childhood trauma which I did not remember. I had not previously known that Trauma is encoded in our bodies and influences how we act and behave. It alienates us from ourselves and the different parts of ourselves from each other. Trauma is about the child being frozen and stuck in the past because the resilient process has not been brought about by a loving, caring parent who cuddles and consoles the child at the time. The resulting immobility and rage are biologically driven and not something of which one should be ashamed.

Because they are unable to trust other people to give them the support they need, these children as adults use a variety of behaviours which do not need other people's support such as using alcohol or other drugs, self-starvation or binging or purging on food, in order to numb themselves and not feel, anything.

Trauma is a disorder of one's capacity to live in the here and now and to engage with other human beings, which is intrinsically self-calming and gives one a sense of belonging and of safety. Being shut down greatly diminishes the children's capacity to feel safe and feel emotionally connected and supported and they may experience self-blame, shame, low self- esteem and loss of real feelings.

When traumatic implicit memories are triggered, they experience overwhelming feelings and impulses. A feeling of danger is interpreted as "I am in danger" in the present when the danger had been experienced in the past.

Feelings of dread, apprehension, depression and yearning to die, self - loathing and feeling helpless, feelings of rage and feeling the need to escape can all be triggered by implicit memories of trauma. I have experienced all of these feelings especially since I have stopped repressing them or suppressing them by overeating and I am able to cope better with these feelings now that I understand their origin. Dr Fisher says in her Self Harm and Suicidality Paper that when distressed, most children seek connection with others, preferably adults, to find reassurance and comfort.

Children who have experienced neglect or abuse have learned to avoid connection, rather than seek it and rely almost exclusively on their own resources.

I remember being smacked by my mother and by my father at my mother's instigation. I do not remember how it felt and I did not cry, so I probably dissociated myself. I do not remember feeling that I could go to either of my parents to be comforted or consoled. I do not remember feeling safe except when I was comforting myself by eating large amounts of refined carbohydrates then feeling ashamed of myself for having done so.

Dr Fisher says that blaming yourself by feeling ashamed is safer than blaming your parents. She says an understanding compassionate, empathic therapist can be the parent the person needed to have as a child. Failing to find such a person, one can be one's own therapist and repair the shame and hurt as good parents would have done.

I decided to be my own therapist with information I gained at the seminar as my guide. I started by being more mindful. Dr Fisher says being mindful is a way of being your own best friend. Being mindful is to be curious and not judgemental as you focus on the flow of your thoughts, feelings and body sensations. Living in the present and focusing on each moment regulates the feeling of emptiness and restores feelings of power and control over your own experience. If you show compassion and love towards all your child parts, your body will respond with warmth and openness. If the Adult self understands the child parts and their unmet needs, the inner child will no longer feel rejected.

To connect with one's child parts one needs to be interested and curious. We have to listen and hear what these parts are trying to tell us and believe that all our distressing feelings, thoughts and behaviours are communications from our own self.

By looking at the photograph of when I was three and comparing it with the photo of when I was three and a half (and I looked more like a four and a half year old) I can see the trauma must have occurred during that time span.

When we returned to Sydney just before I turned three I lost my grandmother who stayed in Greece. I lost my father who resumed his business activities and was no longer available to me. I also lost my mother when she went into hospital to have the baby.

I do not know who looked after me during the time (usually ten days) that my mother spent in hospital. As we had been shown at College, a video of other children's reactions after they had been separated from their mothers for some time, I assume I too would have rejected my mother on her return. Her having been away in itself would have been traumatic however with the new baby to look after and being who she was, I feel my mother was not capable of healing the disconnect between us. As I had not been comforted or consoled, I stayed stuck in my feeling of my having been abandoned by her and of my having been replaced by my sister from then on.

The most traumatic incident at that time was the one my older cousin told me about when I was a teenager. She told me while my mother was in hospital my father had left me at their place overnight. She said "You cried and screamed as your father went out of the front door. Then you threw yourself onto the floor and kept kicking the front door, crying and sobbing until you exhausted yourself and fell asleep and then we put you to bed."

This incident fits exactly into the right time frame for it to be the forgotten trauma which I believe was the prime cause of my binge eating disorder. I had forgotten being told about it and when I remembered it after I had been to the Seminar, I realised how important it could have been and thought about it for some time.

Then as my adult self I picked up my little three year old self, hugged her and told her I understood why she was so upset—that her daddy would pick her up in the morning after she had had a sleep and I would stay with her until she went to sleep. I told her mummy would be home soon and was going to bring her a baby sister whom she could hold and help feed and take for walks with mummy and later play with her when she was older.

I told her I was her friend and I was there to look after her and keep her safe. I held her tight until she had calmed down and I felt upset and warm and loving at the same time. I had created a healing narrative with which I now feel comfortable even though I know it is not true.

Ever since I comforted my three year old self I have been able to control my eating most of the time. Since then, I have been able to limit the carbohydrate grams I eat so I have lost the five kilos I had been unable to lose for so many years. To me it is like a miracle that I am able to buy clothing marked "S" or "XS" even though I still feel large and heavy- not smaller and lighter.

I wear size 10 to 12 clothes and all my 14 to 16 clothes I put in The Smith Family Clothing Bin because they were too big for me. I still have my "bad carb days" after which I feel I have regained the five kilos overnight, however I know what triggers them and accept them as normal for me - especially when I am hungry and buy high carb food.

Dr Fisher says to overcome the forgotten trauma and bring about healing one has to separate oneself from one's symptoms and I feel that is what I have now been able to do. The psycho-analyst I had consulted in Wellington had said to me "The fat will be the last thing to go" so I assumed it ultimately would go.

I did not realise how long it would take or how hard it would be. I am amazed and I regret it has taken so long for me to be able to acknowledge and accept my feelings of abandonment, rejection, sadness, hurt, fear, anger and rage and be able to express them in writing instead of swallowing them and burying them with food.

I feel very grateful for the help especially my ex lecturer, the "good psychologist" and attending Dr Janine Fisher's seminar have given me. For me forgiving and forgetting does not work. It has taken me a long time to take my feelings out of the emotional desert in which I had kept them buried. For me, maintaining the rage by being constantly aware of my anger and its cause is the way I am now able to keep my over-eating under control most of the time.

Underneath the emotional desert, I have found a minefield of frustration and rage which not only affects me but also affects Jim. He had previously told me how my leaving him in Wellington and sending the engagement ring back to him by post had affected him. After his having had a dream recently, he told me about that again with passion, in the middle of the night and also how he felt about my leaving him with all the children, for three days and not telling anyone where I was going.

I am not sorry I did either, however I do regret the effect of my leaving for three days had on our youngest child who told me how distressed she was because she feared she would never see her mother again. I do not know how my temporary disappearance affected the other children as it was not discussed at the time or ever since.

I know I had a very hard time with the three younger children and I gave them a very hard time too. I very much regret and apologise for doing so. Our second youngest daughter told me she had had a" horrible childhood " as I had never told her I loved her and had pushed her away when she came to me for comfort on one occasion. She told me she forgives me and has put it all behind her.

She refused to talk about it or itemise everything that had upset her, which I asked her to do because I felt it would benefit both of us. She said she does not want to go backwards and it is better if she just forgets about it and her father agreed with her. Our three younger children were planned and wanted children. I shudder to think what sort of childhood they would have experienced had they been unwanted children and I had been a single mother!

I am happier now Jim has finally been able to talk about his feelings and express his anger. He felt more real and genuine to me then, than he had ever been since we were married. I marvel at his ability to always appear to be willingly doing what he really does not want to be doing and never talking about how he really feels except on the one occasion.

I am sure this contributed to my feeling empty and unhappy and that I was not living only existing in an emotional desert. Nevertheless throughout the years he has been steadfastly there for all of us and has not only been able to meet all the demands made on him he went the extra mile. I acknowledge how much I am indebted to him and how much I appreciate his ever present support.

I could not have done what I felt was important for me to do or was destined to do, without his help. Had I not married Jim I doubt I could have gone to University, done all the courses I wanted to do, been able to take breaks at the health farm and time out to study and had seven children. One thing I most certainly could not have done was to write this book. I am grateful and glad I was able to write it because it benefited me so much.

Time Marches On—as my father often used to say. One friend from my childhood recently said to me " I don't worry about getting older because as I am getting older so is everyone else." I like her attitude. I have read that Biological age is more important than Chronological age in any case and my father is a good example of a person who was younger in biological age than he was in chronological age. He was young at heart and stayed generous, positive, interested, curious, enthusiastic and involved throughout his seventy nine years of life. Members of my family who keep telling me I have wasted my time writing this book as nobody will read it are wrong! I did not set out to write a best seller. I wrote it as therapy and I have achieved what I set out to achieve.

Even though the book may be personal, private and written about an era in a world which no longer exists, by my having had it published, people who are not offended or harmed, may identify with some aspects of my experience and also benefit from my having written this book. This possibility is available, in the final analysis, only because my father was the kind of person he was for which I remain forever grateful.

According to an ABC News Report on the 28th March 2015, the Premier of Victoria Daniel Andrews announced at the Labor Party state conference in Melbourne that under new rules being introduced by the State Government, Victorian Government board appointments must be at least 50 per cent women.

The 50 per cent quota will also apply to the courts in a bid to encourage more women to join the judiciary.

According to Wikipedia he is a devout Catholic who when he was Health Minister during the passing of the Abortion Law reform Act 2008 disregarded the advice of the Senior Church clergy that it was contrary to the Church teaching.

He is obviously disregarding the Church teaching on the role of women based on the Genesis 2 version of the creation too by introducing these new rules which are in keeping with the Genesis 1 version—a huge step forward in the promotion of equality of opportunity for men and women.

10

FURTHER UPDATES

Like Dame Nellie Melba, I thought I was finished (in her case with Singing and in my case with Writing) however I did not like the way I ended my book and I did not like the front cover so because of some persuasive encouragement, I decided to make those changes in this edition.

Although I still feel uncomfortable and anxious about my making my private history public, I feel better about it now a friend told me an older woman who had read my book told him she had gained more help from having read my book than she had from years of therapy. I would feel even better if I had achieved my main purpose in self -publishing which was to tell other people about the existence of the Genesis Chapter 1 as a separate creation story. No one who has given me feedback after reading my book has commented on Genesis Chapter 1 except my ex lecturer who told me he agrees that Genesis 1 is less sexist than Genesis 11 but he is not sure he agrees with me in all my interpretations of it. When I told a friend I was disappointed about the lack of interest in Genesis Chapter 1 he suggested I write how I feel about it and that is why I am revising the book—again by adding another chapter. He also told me that the younger generations have not been influenced by religious doctrine to the extent I and members of my generation have been. My ex lecturer told me in his letter that he often heard adult clients talking about the fear of hell which was instilled in them by early teaching and how it sits uneasily in the back of their minds. It is only since I have been looking at the Inside Helen that I realised how much I have been adversely affected by this teaching too. I remembered as a teenager wishing and praying I would die before I had committed any mortal sin.

I feel I was very damaged by all the religious teaching I received at school. I know some parents feel their children benefit from attending Christian Doctrine classes however because of my own experience I strongly disagree with them. I feel children would benefit more from attending ethics classes and sexual education classes which not only advise them on safety issues but emphasise the importance of treating women with respect as equals, with consideration of their different needs and by having sex only within a loving consensual relationship.

On the 25th August 2015 on page 3 of the Sydney Morning Herald is an article by Rachel Browne on evidence given by a retired Catholic bishop to the Royal Commission. He said that the Vatican failed to show leadership on the issue of clerical sexual abuse and the present leader Pope Francis has also failed to show authority on this issue. The retired bishop Geoffrey Robinson told of his frustration in seeking assistance with drafting a protocol on sex abuse allegations within the church as no one wanted to touch this subject. Even when he made an approach on a couple of occasions to government, he got nowhere, he said.

In my opinion, just as it suited the Catholic Church to cover up the clerical sexual abuse for decades, it has also suited the church to cover up the existence of Genesis Chapter 1 as a separate story and base all its teachings on the truth of Genesis Chapter 2& 3. Through doing this, it discriminated against women and fostered distrust of women and misogyny for centuries.

On August 26th 2015 on p10 of the Sydney Morning Herald there was an article by Daisy Dumas headed Domestic violence 'National scourge' MEN UNITE ON WOMEN'S SIDE TO BRING CHANGE. Retired Lieutenant-General David Morrison said that two women have been killed every week this year by their partner or former partner and these domestic violence fatalities are a national scourge. He said that had two soldiers been killed every single week in an area of military operations, commanders would be held to account and asked to explain.

As they were all shocked at the scale of the problem of domestic violence the men present, who included male leaders such as ASX head Elmer Funke Kupper, Qantas chief Alan Joyce and Commonwealth boss Ian Narev, the article says, have a plan to use their combined influence to call for gender equality in all sectors of their organisations. The call, it said, comes on the same day as the UN Secretary-General's monthly UNITE Orange Day which is seeking to raise awareness of violence against women.

On the list of goals of the UN Foundation which are due to be ratified at the end of September, the fifth on the list is to achieve gender equality and empower all women and girls by 2030.

Before the Royal Commission into Institutional sexual abuse of children nobody could have imagined the amount of sexual abuse to which children were subjected. Before the statistics about Domestic violence were released, nobody realised the extent of domestic violence in Australia so nothing was done about either.

Until I read chapter 16 of The Closing of the Western Mind. The Rise of faith and Fall of Reason by Charles Freeman, I wondered why the only version of the creation story told by the church is the Genesis 2 Adam and Eve version when Genesis Chapter 1 is also in the Bible.

I now believe the Church chose to keep power in the hands of the men and control over their congregations by making sex a sin by keeping the separate existence of Genesis Chapter 1 a secret. It suited the church which in the Fourth Century AD was establishing the church, to base all its teachings on the truth of Genesis 2 and 3 as their potential for creating wealth, power and control was far greater than that of Genesis chapter 1.

As there are said to be over a billion Roman Catholics in the world, how can gender equality and empowerment of all women and girls be achieved by 2030 if the Catholic and other Christian churches continue to teach that a Male God created Adam in His Image, took his rib to create Eve as a companion for him and because Eve then tempted Adam to break God's commandment, women are the source of all evil, were cursed by God and condemned to being ruled over by their husbands and do not mention Genesis Ch1 ?

I believe this version is an early creation story which was supplanted by the more evolved story in Genesis Chapter 1 which states that men and women were made at the same time in the image of a male and female God who blessed them and told them to be fruitful and multiply and replenish the earth and subdue it: The evidence is in the Bible and the church can no longer cover it up by treating Genesis Chapter 1 as part of Genesis Chapter 2 and 3. If the Papacy could not be relied upon to expose the sexual abuse caused by its clergy how could it be relied upon to expose the reason for its demonization of women or change any of its harmful teachings including on sexuality, gender, homosexuality, same sex marriage, contraception, abortion and euthanasia? The only way to ensure that the innate equality of men and women is recognised is through more Education.

According to an ABC News Report, updated 21st August 2015, the way religion is taught in Victorian primary schools was overhauled by the Victorian Andrews Government after a report found that the Education department guidelines were being breached by the key provider of SRI, Access Ministries. Victoria also banned religious organisations from running prayer groups, handing out Bibles and delivering other unauthorised information sessions in state schools during school hours. As of next year, state school students will not be able to study specialist religious instruction (SRI) during class time and will instead have to do the study before or after school or during lunch time.

Only 20 per cent of students participate in religious education on an opt-in basis and currently the 80% of children who do not attend SRI are prohibited from undertaking any curriculum work during that time. According to this ABC News Report, the Opposition is angry that the Andrews government has broken what it considers to be a pre-election promise, by removing religious instruction from state schools. The Education Minister said he understood that some parents would be angry about the decision but it was the right thing to do. I believe it is in the best interests of children that all Australian states withstand pressure from the Christian lobby and follow the example of Victoria;

In any case I can now see that regardless of whether or not the Christian Churches acknowledge the separate existence of Genesis Chapter 1 and change what they teach, they cannot stop the March of Time in the twenty first century. The Christian churches no longer have the power over people's lives which they had when they were the most educated people in the community.

The greater the level of education in the community the lesser the power of the church will be.

In May 2015 in the mainly Catholic Ireland, the majority of people voted Yes in a referendum on the legalisation of same sex marriage making Ireland the first country in the world to do so.

The US Supreme Court in June 2015 ruled 5 to 4 that the Constitution provides same sex couples the right to marry. Marriage Equality now exists throughout the United States.

In Australia the matter is still on "hold" because the former Prime Minister Abbott is firmly of the view that the traditional view of marriage is right and will not allow a conscience vote in his party regarding the legalisation of same sex marriage. Despite this, change is inevitable because of the changing of public opinion. Who would have imagined even ten years ago that on the 15th August 2015 the local paper Wentworth Courier (established in 1947) would have on page 3, a photo of four fathers, three of whom were each holding a baby and one of whom was carrying a young child, with the heading "DADDY DAYCARE"? These fathers are part of a new group called "Bondi Fathers" who enjoy each other's company while they are looking after their children on the weekends. This to me demonstrates how far society has moved on from the traditional Adam and Eve type of gender roles to behaving more in accordance with the innate equality of men and women as demonstrated in the Genesis Chapter 1 version of the creation.

I have quoted verbatim Genesis Chapter 1 in the first chapter of my book and Genesis Chapter 2 & 3 in the sixth chapter of my book. I have explained why there are two versions of the creation in the Bible and I have compared them. I have written about what I feel are the consequences of belief in the truth of the Genesis chapter 2&3 and of not being aware of the separate existence of Genesis Chapter 1.

I learned about the power of the mind when I left school and went to the Kindergarten Teachers Training College. I remember reading a story about a man who grew beautiful tomatoes near his neighbour's fence and so the neighbour would not be tempted to eat them told him they were only ornamental and were poisonous. When a visitor to the neighbour's house ate a tomato and was told it was poison the visitor died (probably of a heart attack) because he believed what he was told. I feel that what one believes is very powerful and has serious consequences. That is why I feel it is so important that all Christian children are told there are two creation stories in the Bible not one.

By looking up the Internet I found an article under the name "What place for the Catholic Church in the 21st century Australia?" by Judy Courtin---- a then PhD student in the Faculty of Law at Monash University, called: THE CONVERSATION. 20th June 2013. From reading this Article I learned that as borne out by statistics, the Catholic Church in Australia, with about half a million members, has been a greatly diminished force in society and the reasons for such a decline are many. There has been a 67% reduction from 1966 to 2009 in the number of nuns, brothers and priests (not including the diocesan priests). Many Catholics no longer support the institutional church and many have become people of no religion because they feel that many Catholic doctrines no longer fit a modern western society. There has also been the emergence of the sexual abuse crisis which has brought about the great exodus of the clergy and the faithful from the Catholic

Church. Many people also feel dissatisfied with the gender issue that the men will not allow women priests.

The men who established the Catholic Church were obviously very astute business men as the article says the Catholic Church is the biggest private employer in Australia. With 180,000 employees it makes A$15 billion a year from education, health and welfare services. It is reported to own A $100 billion worth of properties and other assets and receives hundreds of millions of dollars each year by way of donations from parishioners. It has a tax free status like other religious organisations. All its investment earnings are tax free and it does not pay rates for its properties or pay land tax or capital gains tax on the sale of assets. The author of the article says that the extraordinary wealth of the Catholic Church contributes to its power, a power and wealth, she says, many believe should attract the status of a corporation and attract tax status like any other big business.

I must say I have spent time in St Vincent's Emergency myself and with Jim and we have each been patients in both the Public and the Private St Vincent's Hospitals. I trust the Catholic Church makes a great deal of money running them as in my opinion it deserves every single cent. The atmosphere is both busy and efficient as well as relaxed and friendly. The multi cultural men and women Doctors and Nurses are attentive, kind and caring so the experience of being in hospital has been as pleasant and enjoyable as is possible.

All the men in the Vatican exist because their mothers brought them into the world. Perhaps it is now time for the Catholic Church to acknowledge without women they would not be alive, stop treating Sex as Sin, accept women as equal human beings with equal rights and adjust the basis of its teachings by including the further evolved story of the creation in Genesis chapter 1. If the Catholic Church is not willing to change, society is already moving in this direction and the Catholic Church will be left behind.

When there was a change of government in Australia on the 7th September 2013 I was angry there was only one woman in the cabinet. On the 14th September this year 2015, Malcolm Turnbull, former leader of the liberal opposition, challenged Tony Abbott for the Leadership of the Liberal party and won.

There were then five women in cabinet. One hundred million dollars has been pledged to tackle Domestic Violence and raise the level of respect for women. However in May 2016 the Prime Minister called a double dissolution election on July 2 and the government was returned with a majority of only one seat.

Nevertheless I am optimistic that belief in the superiority of men based on acceptance of the truth of the Adam and Eve myth is being changed to belief in the innate equality of men and women based on the truth of Genesis Ch.1 in the hearts and minds of all Australians sooner rather later because the Prime Minister Turnbull's Department is enquiring into whether there is equality of opportunity to achieve one's potential in the PM&C Department and whether there is any unconscious bias against women. I trust the bias against women in the Church's choosing the Genesis Ch 2&3 version of the creation story instead of Genesis Ch 1 will be made evident to everyone and demands for change will be made in the interest of Truth and Justice.

I started my inner journey into Why Am I So Angry? and My Search for the Truth in 2013.

There have been many changes since then both in the wide world and also in my private world.

During 2017 Jim had tripped on a bath mat and was taken to St Vincent's Emergency because he had gashed the back of his head and fractured his ribs by falling onto the edge of the bath.

The doctors warned me he might not survive.

When he collapsed in our GP's waiting room a few weeks later the ambulance again took him to St Vincent's Emergency.

We were all very concerned about his welfare as he was getting less mobile and sleeping more during the day. Although Jim always said "I'm staying home. I'm not going anywhere" we were all very relieved when he agreed to go for two weeks Respite Care at Mark Moran Vaucluse.

The St Vincent's Community Palliative Care Team had visited him at home and told us they would also visit him in Vaucluse. They saw him during our second week there and told us he did not need palliative care yet but was close and they did not know how long he would live if he completely stopped eating.

The first few days he had his meals in the dining room with Connie and me.

Then he had meals in his room and sometimes he ate very little and stayed in bed.

On the 22nd September 2017 Jim had not been eating for two days and had been sleeping almost all the time.

About ten O'clock I told him I was going to breakfast with Connie and I would not be long.

As we were going into the dining room Adam came past us on his way to see his father.

I am not sure how long it was before he came into the dining room and said " Mum you need to come with me because Dad has gone."

When I went into our bedroom Gifty, Michael, Rozi and Trish were there.

I went back and asked Connie to come with me.

We both sat at Jim's bedside and looked at him and he looked as if he was asleep.

I kept touching his face which was warm.

I did not believe he had died until the house doctor examined him about 11.30am and then I knew it was true. As Jim wanted to be cremated, the doctor filled out the Death Certificate and also one regarding the cremation.

Trish wanted Maia to say good bye to her grandfather after school so Michael rang Walter Carter and asked them to come after 4pm which they did.

We all left the room then I went back and watched while they put his clothes in a black plastic bag.

One of the men asked me was I a religious person and I said "no."

He asked me did I want to say goodbye so I kissed Jim on the cheek and this time his face was very cold.

They put him on a stretcher and covered him from head to toe in red velvet.

It did not take long. They took the Death Certificate with them.

I decided to stay at Vaucluse until the end of the weekend.

We went to the Walter Carter office on Monday morning after Rozi had taken me home and we made the arrangements for the funeral to be held at 11am on Wednesday 27th September.

Adam rang the Leagues Club to reserve lunch for twenty people at 12.30pm and had also arranged a video to be made of photos to be shown at the funeral.

Jim did not want his death notice to be published until after his funeral so Jim's Death Notice appeared in the Sydney Morning Herald on Saturday 30th September 2017.

GERONDIS, JAMES DENNIS

Former Pharmacist of Bondi Junction - a born athlete and lover of sport, especially Golf, Easts Roosters and All Blacks Rugby, stopped breathing on the morning of the twelfth day of a two week respite at Mark Moran Vaucluse on Friday 22nd September 2017.

He had been well cared for by the compassionate nursing staff and lovingly supported by his wife Helen and sister Connie, both also living at Mark Moran Vaucluse at the time, as well as other members of his family especially Rozi, Adam and Michael.

Jim had a peaceful and painless death after slowing down over the last nine months - giving up two of his greatest pleasures, Golf and driving his car- and becoming increasingly immobile.

His request for a private cremation was carried out on the 27th September 2017.

He will always be remembered for his kindness and willingness to help others, his sense of humour and his devotion to his family.

He will be sadly missed by everyone who knew him.

Walter Carter

Jim's Funeral was on WEDNESDAY 27TH SEPTEMBER 2017

This is some of what I wrote about it in my notebook.

"I took the large photo of the Wellington Cable Car from under the glass in the Dining room and our Wax Orange Blossoms tied with white ribbons from our Wedding Ceremony and the Photo of Jim Adam had framed and we went to Walter Carter's about ten thirty.

We had plenty of time to decorate the coffin which looked attractive because it was painted a light wood colour.

Michael started the proceedings by announcing at 11 am that Maia would be playing her own composition "Hope" on her violin and it was beautiful, vibrant and warm.

Then the photos were shown for about ten minutes and they were all good photos and everyone there was included in them with Jim.

Jacqui went to the podium to support James and Lucy when each of them spoke briefly followed by Luke looking very handsome and professional in his suit and then Beth who was also emotional like Lucy and brief and the whole thing lasted about twenty minutes.

It ended with Fred Astaire singing "Dancing Cheek to Cheek."

On the way out I said to the man in charge "That must have been one of the shortest Funerals you have ever had" and he said "Almost. We had one man at his father's funeral who said 'Goodbye Dad' and that was it."

Everyone came home briefly then we went to the Club where I gave the man my card and he scanned everyone's Driving Licences and we all went up to the restaurant.

The two long tables at the back of the room had "Reserved" notices on them.

One of the attendants brought a biro and two pages of paper for everyone to write down their choice for lunch.

Beth came with me to the counter and read the lists to the cashier who read it all back then tapped my credit card and we all had our lunch within twenty minutes."

Later in the afternoon Adam took my computer to Vaucluse to show Connie the photo video which she watched intently. She was always very close to her brother and I felt that allowed her to share and be part of his funeral which was a good idea.

Adam also emailed the photo video to Lilian who watched it with the help of her granddaughter Vanessa. Lil told me she thought Adam had made a good job of selecting the photos and I agreed with her.

I know my sister and other relatives and friends of his were upset about being excluded however it was the small close family funeral Jim had asked for in his will.

Our eldest son Denny flew down from Queensland.

Beth our second daughter flew up from Melbourne with her partner Catharine.

Beth's son Luke came by train from Newcastle.

Jim's sister Celia flew from Wellington with her daughter Diona.

Michael & Jacqui and their grown up children Lucy and James— Rozi and Colin and grown up children Jordan, James and Jack— Adam and his wife Gifty and Trish with her eleven year old daughter all live in Sydney and were the only other people present.

While waiting for Walter Carter on Friday I had phoned his cousin Spiro and his friend Con, with both of whom he used to enjoy having coffee at the club until he could not walk that far.

I also rang my sister and my cousin Juanita.

Anita rang to tell me she would come to see me at Vaucluse and she did.

Before the funeral Denny had picked up Jim's wedding ring from the jeweller who made it smaller to fit my finger. It looks beautiful under my wedding ring which I had had made from one of his mother's sovereigns and it comforts me whenever I look at it.

Jim died just before Rozi went on holiday and she seemed to make it her priority to look after me until she went back to work. When Beth was here she helped her with cleaning out the drawers and Rozi enthusiastically cleaned the cupboards inside as well as outside.

She took me for drives and shopping and for lunch.

She, Michael and Adam seemed to have an agreement that at least one of them would contact me every day and make sure I was alright and find out what I had been doing.

As well as a small family funeral Jim said in his will he wanted half of his ashes to be scattered according to the wishes of the majority of his wife and his children and the other half be taken to New Zealand to be scattered under a tree in Mt Victoria Wellington.

When Jim made his will I feel he assumed his sister Celia who lives in Wellington would be at his funeral and would be able to take the ashes back to Wellington when she returned home.

I do not think he would have anticipated that his ashes would not be ready in time for that to happen and a separate trip would have to be made.

Adam and Gifty invited us to Brunch at their home on Sunday 22nd October and some of Jim's ashes were scattered around their large Olive Tree after we had eaten.

Adam had made me a delicious Mushroom Frittata with no salt which I appreciated very much.

When we went outside to the Olive tree Adam gave me a spoon full of ashes to scatter under the tree which I did not like doing and only did so because I felt it was important to Adam that I did.

Michael, Rozi, Beth and Anita decided they would go to Wellington to scatter the other half of Jim's ashes on Friday 27th October 2017.

I did not want to have anything more to do with Jim's ashes however Rozi talked me into going.

Beth flew up from Melbourne to meet us at the Airport so she could come to Wellington on the same flight.

Anita our niece and only God-child also met us at the Airport.

Michael, Rozi and I, Jim's executors and trustees, waited for both of them at the Airport.

We were there for what seemed like hours because the flight had been delayed for an hour.

The flight to Wellington was very bumpy and I was very happy when we landed.

The whole thing could have been a disaster.

Thanks to Diona, Alex and Celia we all knew exactly where to go in Mt Victoria.

Michael, Anita, Rozi and Beth all walked up the hill while Alex took Nick to Plimmer Park.

Diona took me and Celia to the park too and Celia tried to walk but was in pain and had to stay in the car.

Nick and I sat on a stone bench in Plimmer Park.

The tree was further up and too hard for us to get there. We could see them scattering the ashes around the tree from where we were sitting. It was 6pm and the twilight had just started.

It was especially good that Anita came to Wellington too. She was part of Jim's life even before she was born. Connie, her mother chose me to be her Godmother I felt because I shared her morning sickness for three days on a ship on the way to Wellington for her surprise trip home.

Everything, including the weather, seemed to be perfect.

Mt Victoria and Plimmer Park were beautiful and uplifting and I was glad I was there too.

Our farewell dinner for Jim was at one of his favourite restaurants, Little India, where Celia had booked a table for ten with an empty chair at each end of the long table— one for Jim and one for his friend Bernie his only friend who was at our wedding and with whom he had had a very long association.

Celia was still in pain but she managed to do most of the talking and the atmosphere was warm and friendly.

We were all very pleased everything went so well.

On Jim's birthday, 28th December, we marked the occasion with brunch at Adam and Gifty's home. Michael and his nephew James played nine holes of golf at the Australian Golf Club that afternoon and Michael scattered the remainder of Jim's ashes which amounted to a couple of hands full around Jim's favourite areas.

The golf course was at its best as the competitions had just ended and the sun was shining.

We were very pleased we had done everything according to Jim's wishes and we felt he would have approved of the choices we had made.

During the five years it has taken me to finally finish my book my feelings have changed.

I am no longer an angry person.

I watched the TV on the Saturday 9th December 2017 when Parliament erupted into joyful and enthusiastic applause when the Marriage Equality Bill was passed.

It came into effect throughout Australia on Tuesday January 9th 2018.

I am happy the Royal Commission on Institutional Child Abuse which gave so many victims the opportunity to be heard and to be believed has finished and the report was released in December.

I was not surprised that 62.8% of the victims who complained were about Catholic Institutions.

I am happy that after debating across both houses of parliament for more than 100 hours, Victoria became the first state in Australia to legalise Assisted Dying for the terminally ill even though it will not come into effect until 2019.

Because of the recent changes in the law it seems to me we are becoming a more compassionate society on many levels.

I still do not understand why in a modern society Christians are still allowed to tell children the Adam and Eve version of the creation which makes sex a sin and discriminates in favour of men and against women and ignore the more evolved Genesis Ch 1 version also in the Bible.

I am no longer angry about this because I now understand most teachers have no choice but to teach what they have been told to teach.

Though I still believe this needs to change in order to protect future generations in this generation it appears that women are taking control of the situation by publicly complaining about what they consider to be inappropriate behaviour to them from men in all walks of life.

I am very glad women are courageous enough to expose these men and set the record straight instead of suffering in silence as they used to do.

I became concerned that because of the right to Freedom of Religion, Christians may try to continue to tell children Homosexuality is Abnormal and Abhorrent to God and marriage is only be between a man and a woman when I heard talk about amendments after the changed law was passed.

I am not angry about it however I feel the time has come for this to be prohibited by law.

Despite the right to Freedom of Religion female circumcision is a crime in Australia.

In my opinion mentally harming children also needs to be made a crime in Australia.

It makes no sense to me that boys who are told the Adam and Eve version they were made in God's image and girls were only created for their benefit, would not think boys are superior to girls and would not think as men they are entitled to use women for their own benefit, needs and desires whether or not the woman consents and thereafter could find themselves in prison for years if the woman proved beyond reasonable doubt she did not consent.

The most important change in me I feel is that I am no longer angry with Jim.

I was happy when I looked through Jim's 2008 diary and he had referred to when we had spent our Wedding Anniversary in Chatswood at a modern hotel with a large sunny studio room and a King size comfortable bed. I was down in weight and felt glamorous in my new short crimson nightie.

We were there alone, the two of us, not only with no other people but without the intervention of other interests particularly sport on TV.

The togetherness which was missing on our first honeymoon was very much there this time and I wondered why.

I felt maybe we had both changed for the better.

Jim says in his Diary "This Honeymoon was what honeymoons are supposed to be like —at last."

That meant to me that he had not liked our first honeymoon either though he did not say so.

I felt that despite his mother's treating her sons and daughters as equals Jim had been adversely influenced by some of his Catholic Education and especially the Adam & Eve story, as I had been.

He had never let us discuss our first honeymoon nor had he ever apologised for it.

I had never been able to forgive him until I understood how much he had been influenced by his Catholic Education and particularly being told the Adam and Eve Story even though he has always denied being influenced by any religious teaching because of his Mother's attitude.

My experience with him proved to me that was not so.

On reflection I wonder why I ever thought he would relate to me in any way other than the way in which he did. I thought it was because he did not like me or my company.

Now I realise it was not personal.

In my opinion it was caused by what he was taught about women in his Catholic schools.

I feel by my writing and publishing my book I have not only benefited myself.

Despite his telling me it has been a complete waste of time I feel it has benefited him and our relationship too and for that I am forever grateful.

The reason I had my book published was because everyone seemed to know about Adam & Eve and nobody seemed know the more evolved story of the creation which is also in the Bible.

I still think this is important however I am no longer angry about it because it seems to me more men and women are now treating each other as equals both at work and at home especially as parents. It warms my heart to see increasing numbers of men with their babies, toddlers or young children whenever I visit a shopping centre.

I believe the message in Genesis Ch 1 is gradually replacing the message in Genesis Ch 2 & 3 in the psyches of Australian men and women because they are less influenced by the churches now they know how priests and brothers treated the children in their care and how the abuse was covered up order to protect the churches.

I am glad I have now come to the end of the last update of this book.

I am grateful and feel blessed to have a loving family and extended family and my own home.

I am especially grateful to Denny for his support of my book.

Michael, Rozi and Adam for their caring support of me after Jim had died.

Beth, Trish and Jenny who is so far away, and Connie, Celia and Lilian for their concern.

Anita for her telephone support and for the lunches when Jim was present and now he is not.

Nicholas for his continuing interest in my book.

Juanita, Katie, Clio and the other relatives and friends who keep in touch with me.

Every reader I have had or may have in the future,

My ex-lecturer without whom this book would not have been written.

The Good Psychologist.

The people who have been kind and helpful to me throughout my life, especially my Aunty Mary. And Jim without whom I would not have been able to do what I wanted and needed to do in my life and without whom I feel so very alone.

Even though I wear smaller size clothes and am no longer angry at how I look, I have decided once my book has been republished I need to improve my fitness.

I enrolled in a couple of fitness classes starting in February at the Community & Seniors Club.

I feel this is my last chance to improve my fitness and also meet other people.

One of the classes includes social dancing with or without a partner.

The Good Psychologist says in her Report about me " Indoctrinated in the Catholic faith, you believed your suffering was your own fault while your identity refused to accept this.

I believe you resolved this essential split by developing your mind at the expense of your body."

I feel now is the time to pay more attention to my body while I am still in it.

I asked one of my friends how long did it take her to get over the death of her husband and she said "You never get over it. You just learn to adapt."

I do not feel I have adapted very well so far.

I never saw Jim as an old man.

I always saw him as the young handsome man, well ahead of me in looks, that I had married.

I do not like living alone. I was very pleased my cousin Marian stayed with me for five days.

The only time I had lived alone was when Jim was in hospital after his three or four operations.

Looking back through my life I realise I am a "night person" and how frustrating it has been ever since I was a teenager to have to stay home at night when I have wanted to go out.

I have read or was told that should DNA be taken when a child is born it is possible to predict how long that child will live and what will cause his or her death.

I do not know if this is true.

Assuming it is true and my time to die has not yet come, I trust that once I have started to attend the dancing and other fitness class I will then be able to better adapt to my loss and feel better.

Some people have urged me to write another book.

I felt I had no choice but to write this one and I am glad I have persevered until the end.

I feel that "Enough is Enough" because I have achieved what I wanted and needed to achieve by writing this book and I am very glad I did.

I would like to add that in the three part series " Secrets of our Cities" on SBS last year Bondi was featured and my sister and I appeared in one segment of that section talking about our father who was brought into attention again because of the book "Greek Cafes & Milk Bars of Australia" by Effy Alexakis and Leonard Janiszewski.

My sister had given them information and photos about the opening of the first real milk bar in Australia in 1932 and they had used some of this in their book which was launched in the theatre of the State Parliament on the 15th March 2016.

Effy and Leonard are writing another book about the children of the original owners of the Greek Cafes and Milk Bars and are endeavouring to have a Plaque put in Martin Place where the Black and White Milk Bar was established which acknowledgment would be much appreciated by all our family.

THE AUTHOR

HELEN GERONDIS (NEE ADAMS) WAS born in Sydney Australia. She is the elder daughter of a mother born in Athens Greece and a father born in what was then called Greek Thrace, Turkey. She found it difficult to fit in with two different cultures and with a Non-Catholic background, she found it difficult to adjust at the Convent School she attended from Kindergarten to the end of High school.

After school, as she had been told she was not allowed to go to University, she qualified as a Kindergarten Teacher, married, had her first child and studied by Correspondence in order to matriculate and succeeded. With the support of her husband and the help of women child minders she enrolled in the five year Part-time Law Course which took her eight years to complete, during which time they had five more children.

She was one of the first twenty five women to be admitted to the Bar of New South Wales and first Greek Australian woman to do so. She could not practise full time at the Bar because of her family commitments and the unavailability of child care for their seven children. She did other courses, practised whenever she was given Legal Aid briefs and spent as much time in court as possible listening.

When she left the Bar she did a Post Grad Dip. Individual Psychotherapy and Relationship Therapy Course. After graduation, she worked as a Counsellor at a Probation and Parole Office and later as a Volunteer Face to Face Counsellor at Lifeline.

Standing next to the Flower of Remembrance of The Siege
in Martin Place, Sydney on the 16th December 2014
Photo by Jim 16th January 2015